To Janine

My Trayor Sisto for
thank you Suppor
all your
God Bless

Rosann Toppes
7-27-2012

MW01148242

Abuse Hidden Behind the Badge"

BY

ROSAURA TORRES

EDITOR

MICHAEL W. THOMAS

GRAPHIC ARTIST

ANGEL CALO, JR.

"ABUSE HIDDEN BEHIND THE BADGE"

My married name was Rosaura Torres-Sadler.

This is my true story.

The names have been changed to protect the innocent, not necessarily my abusers.

DEDICATION

Dedico este libro a mis hijos y mi hija, a mis nietos, hermanas y hermanos, y a los sobrevivientes de la Violencia Domestica. Hay una luz al final del túnel.

Y as mi madre y padre, Ismael y Carmen Torres, gracia por todas su amor.

Torres Publishing Group LLC
PO Box 5253
Philadelphia, PA 19141
215-758-0338

www.torrespublishing.com

ISBN 1452827346
EAN-13 9781452827346
Library of Congress Catalog Card Number
1-365402318

TORRES PUBLISHING GROUP LLC

CONTENTS

ABUSE HIDDEN BEHIND THE BADGE

I dedicate this book to my children and grandchildren, sisters and brothers and to my Survivors of Domestic Violence. There is a light at the end of the tunnel.

I was born on February 26, 1960 to Jesus Ortiz and Isabella De La Rosa Ortiz. My parents arrived to the land of the free in 1949 from Puerto Rico for the dream that so many of us wished. Most Puerto Rican families would either go to Chicago or New York or even Philadelphia, but not my mother and father, they moved to Milwaukee Wisconsin, where I was born.

I am the youngest daughter of nine children; as my mother would say, I was "The one with the most mouth." In my mother's younger years, she was married, and out of her marriage, my mother gave birth to a little girl.

During my childhood, my mother and I would sit and I would listen to her life from the past. My mother did not show any shame in telling me of her first love. I could close my eyes and see my mother as a young woman. She was so beautiful.

In our family, I always felt that keeping secrets was a must but not my mother, her marriage to her first love must have been remarkable. I would look into her eyes and see the love she felt for her deceased husband. My mother was our storyteller and I was fortunate to know this wonderful lady.

Is it possible to love two different men so strongly? Could you only be in love with one person once in your lifetime with all your heart and the next relationships are just that, relationships? Do you only get one true love? I wish I had the answer!

5

My mother spoke so loving of her first husband; never did she mention his name. You could see the love in her eyes as she spoke of him. Out of their marriage, Mami was blessed with her first-born daughter. I could see the tears in her eyes and she would tell me what happened to her first husband. My mother's husband was murdered in Puerto Rico and she was so proud of him. Mami's first husband was running for a political position in Puerto Rico. How I wish I knew more but she would stop in mid conversation and never continue the story.

Sadly, my oldest sister passed away when she was just an infant. My mother would also speak of her childhood but I was never fortunate enough to have met my grandparents from my mother's side of the family. Just looking at her beautiful, soft and compassionate face, I could see how much pain the death of her first-born caused her. It hurt me deeply. My mother always felt blessed to have given birth to this angel from God that was sent to her.

Many times during my childhood and adult life, I wished I knew when my mother and father met. Was it love at first sight?

Every little girl wants to hear the fairy tale marriage or the happily ever after story. I knew one day I would meet my "Prince Charming"'.

Many times my uncle Jim would remind me of how handsome my father was in his younger days. I could only imagine how mom fell in love with dad because I remember what it was like when I met my husband.

During my childhood, my uncle Jim would record several films of us when I was a child. My memories as a child would be sitting there watching the film and Mami hugging and kissing Papi. Oh, how beautiful their love was.

Rosaura Torres

As the years passed, I never saw the love between my parents for many years. I knew my parents loved each other dearly but my father had a "wandering eye." Wow, he loved the women! In the process, my mother suffered through his extra-marital activities.

I would never be able to answer the question that many of us would want to know. Why do men and woman cheat on one another? Are men and woman afraid of dying alone?

From my parent's marriage, they were blessed with eight children. My second oldest sister died at the age of two. My sister fell down a flight of stairs, which caused her a severe head injury, and she never recovered from the fall.

Oh, how I could see the pain and sorrow in my mother's eyes and how I just wanted to erase all her pain. Mami's heart was broken and to make matters worse, she had already lost her first child.

In more than 60 years of marriage, my mother and father had seven more children: Jordon, Lee Jr., Ralph, Edwina, Marcia, Arturo and myself. When I think about it now I could not understand how Mami did it. Where did she have the strength to endure the struggles of the past?

Papi might have had a wondering eye but he was a wonderful father. Our father loved us and when we were children, Papi would take us to the roller derby, wrestling, and to the Spanish movies. I loved my father dearly and Mami always said you have to forgive because if you don't you will never be able to move forward with your life. My mother forgave our father for whatever took place in their marriage.

We were a poor family but as a child, I did not feel we were poor. I had two loving parents. Mom always made sure that we had a hot meal before we went off to school. Even when we did not have enough, Pop, would say, have some coffee with bread and butter, I was okay with our means. My Brother Lee's memory was that the neighborhood church would help us when we were living in Wisconsin.

Memories of my childhood in Wisconsin were of my siblings and I sleeping on the floor, which was normal, or not having enough to eat. I believed that all families were poor and they all lived in that condition. I was just a little girl. We were poor and always struggling. Even when we moved to Philadelphia, PA, we slept on the floor of my grandmother's apartment.

During the time, we lived in Wisconsin my father worked for American Motors. I could not even begin to imagine how difficult it was for my father especially when he did not speak any English. My father was not raised by his mother because she abandoned him when he was a child. Papi would tell me the story of his childhood and how he and my grandfather would sleep under bridges. Dad was not close to his mother and I am able to say this because my grandmother was not kind to myself and or my siblings. I never knew how it felt to have a grandmother or a grandfather.

We left Milwaukee, Wisconsin in 1963. It was cold when we left and I remember the bus ride to Philadelphia, PA. The majority of the Puerto Ricans who came from Puerto Rico would move to Green Street, Mt. Vernon, or even Callow Hill Street.

I wish I could tell you more about Wisconsin but all that I remember is the snow and the Greyhound bus to the great city of "Brotherly Love." My brother Lee would reminisce about the sad times in Wisconsin. WI. I wondered, "Were there ever any happy times?"

We arrived in Philadelphia and went to my grandmother's apartment, which was located on Mt. Vernon Street. The family of seven all squeezed into a two bedroom apartment.

My grandmother was not a pleasant women and she did not hide her feelings from us. It makes me very sad when I speak of her. My grandmother left this world never showing my brothers, sisters, and I the love of a grandmother.

My mother did not like Philadelphia so we headed back to Wisconsin. We must have been there maybe another two years the most and headed right back to Philly again. I often wondered whether things would have been better for us if we had stayed in Wisconsin.

My parents found an apartment on 19th & Callow Hill Street in 1965. The area at that time was made up of many Hispanic and African American families.

As a child one of my best memories was this little corner store where we would all get our penny candy. Wow! How I remember our Halloween and how our playgrounds were near the large statues near the children's detention center. During the summer, we played in the water fountains of Fairmount Park and never did I feel poor, but we were. I never understood why people treated us differently and why the name-calling.

I was baptized at St Peter's and Paul Cathedral in Logan Circle in 1965. There were many times when I was a child and I would enter the church, look up at the ceiling of the cathedral and felt I was so close to God. As an adult, I realize that God is everywhere.

My first memory of Domestic Violence was on a quiet chilly night back in 1966.

My mother and my other siblings were all sitting around just talking. That horrible night even now still lives with me. I still question people's anger and their abusive behavior.   My Cousin Lucy's stepfather Colon was obsessed with her. This man was just a sick human being and a "pig."

On that night we were all sitting in the living room of our apartment on 19th & and Callow Hill Street. It was Mami, my brother Arturo, Jordon, Edwina, Marcia, and me.

We heard the screams and then we all started to scream. My brother Jordon ran out of the apartment and he found Lucy at the corner of 19th and Callow Hill stabbed by her stepfather. We were crying while my mother was trying her best to calm us down. I could not understand why the

violence was there and the obsession that he had for my
cousin Lucy was scary.

I know in my heart that God was watching over my cousin Lucy because she did survive. Not long after the stabbing, Lucy left her mother's home. I heard later on that her stepfather Colon was never charged or arrested for this horrific crime. What makes this stabbing so disturbing is that it took place on the corner where the Philadelphia 9th police district was located and no one saw or heard a thing. Our apartment was located right in the middle of the block. I remember always saying, "I JUST DON'T GET IT.".

This memory of Domestic Violence lived with me throughout my life and not long after that horrible abuse, we moved to North Philadelphia.

We moved into a three-story house. Oh, how happy we all were about moving to our big house. I was only seven years old and to me it was like moving into a mansion where there was room for all of us.

Sadly, two of my brother's became heroin addicts. This put such a horrible strain on my poor mother. I didn't think her heart could take much more pain.

One particular evening Giovanna, Amber, Little Mary, my sister Edwina, Marcia and me had returned from the movies. As always, we rushed into the kitchen to raid the refrigerator. We stepped into the kitchen and with shock and disbelief we found my brother Ralph lying on the kitchen floor with a needle in his arm. My brother's face was a purple blue and the sight of my brother brought a shock to every part of my body.

I was just a little girl and the only way I knew how to react to what I saw was to scream. My brother Lee was angry with all our screaming. The sight of my brother on the ground caused my mother to have a heart attack. The house was in such turmoil. I often thought and wondered where did my mother get her strength, but I know where I got my strength from. Many years have gone by and surviving the drugs and the gang war back then was just unbelievable. My cousin Jim was visiting and he was shot with a pellet gun. My brother-in-law to be, Manny, was sitting in his car two weeks before his wedding to my sister Edwina and several neighborhood gang members beat him severely; they left him for dead.

As a child, my siblings and I worked in the Blueberry Fields and Peach Farms. I remembered when Mami was up on a tree picking peaches when she slipped and fell directly on her back! I was a little girl trying to help her mother so I ran to assist her. It truly amazed me how she got the strength to pull herself up off the ground.

In today's society children, working on farms would be in violation of the child labor laws, but back in the 1960's many Latino children in our neighborhood worked in the fields. We were taught by our parents to be strong workers. Mom and dad had enough of the gang war and violence so they thought it would be best for the family to relocate to New Jersey. What they didn't realize was that we moved to the area where the riot of 1972 destroyed the city of Camden, New Jersey.

Camden, New Jersey was not such a great place to live in the 1970's. The first night was not so great; it was the summer of 1972. The police threw a tear bomb into our neighborhood without realizing each of us had a box fan in the windows. The gas seeped into the house and when the gas entered the house, we all went running outside. I had never experienced anything like this before.

During my childhood, I loved the Ruiz family that we would always hang out with. Those were best days; I will always remember Mr. Jose Ruiz. He was such a wonderful man and he left me with great memories from my childhood.

Mr. Ruiz was like my second father. At the age of eight, I had an accident and I needed surgery on my right arm. My surgery took place in the summer of 1968 and we used to

spend time at Fairmount Park. There was a lake there called Gustine Lake; this is where we spent our summers. The summer that I had my surgery, I had to wear a huge cast that covered the upper part of my body and I wasn't able to swim. This wonderful man stayed with me as the rest of the children played and splashed around in the pool. Mr. Ruiz didn't want to leave me behind at home.

I will always remember my father working a lot and we did not see much of him. When we did spend time with Papi he would take us to the roller derby and to the wrestling match at the arena in Philadelphia. Mom would tell our Dad to take us because she always thought he was meeting a lady at the shows.

Later in years, my mother finally told us that our father was a rolling stone. In other words, he liked the ladies and he cheated on her a lot, but Dad never left her. Even up until the day my mother went home to God, he stayed by her side. Through all the cheating, my mother never stopped loving my father, and that took a lot of strength from her.

In the year that we moved to Camden, New Jersey, I just started the fifth grade and I met the nicest sisters whose names were Addison and Sara Naives. There was also the Muniz family, the Colon family along with Daisy Torres and her family; these were the families we had a wonderful relationship with. They were like my sisters and I still have the fondest memories of my childhood friends.

We continued through the horrible struggle of my brothers' drug addiction. Each and every one of us was affected. No matter how difficult and disturbing the memories of drug abuse are, I will always love my brothers. You do not turn your back on your family; you love them and pray God will find a way to help them through their struggles.

Years went on and then my mother decided to move to Florida. I was not sure back then, what exactly made my mother relocate there. Mom never said why but I think it had a lot to do with my father's cheating. Mom just couldn't put up with it so we sold all of our things and packed up what we had left. We then moved to Florida.

At first, I didn't like it in Florida. I wanted to go back home because I had a crush on a boy. I was just a kid, but you know how it is with your first love. His name was Jimmy and I remember how young and immature we both were. I can laugh and smile about it now.

I had an accident with my bike when I was fourteen and I noticed something was wrong with my vision. I just thought I needed glasses.

I was diagnosed with a cataract, which I inherited from my grandfather. I was fourteen and this disease is usually for older adults, so I wondered why this happened to me?

My first surgery was performed when I was 14 years old. During that time cataract surgery was not like it is today, I was admitted to the hospital for five days. It was a terrible experience for me. Even the doctors were baffled by my diagnosis because they didn't see cataracts in children my age very often.

Florida had to grow on me, which it did. I guess when you're a kid you can adjust. I was just a teenager and I did miss my friends back home. It was at this time that I experienced my first sexual relationship, I was a kid and I lost my virginity. It wasn't what I expected it to be, so I wasn't happy about it. My first experience felt dirty and I was ashamed.

16

Rosaura Torres

My brother Arturo must have not cared for Florida either, Arturo and one of his young buddies ran away and they got as far as Atlanta, GA. before they were returned home.

Out of nowhere, Mami and Papi decided to move back to Camden, New Jersey, Wow, I never truly understood my parents; it seemed they couldn't make up their minds! I was somewhat happy and kind of sad because I did make new friends in Florida.

Once we were back from Florida, I started dating my old childhood sweetheart. I thought okay, it's going to be much normal, I was starting to attended High School and I was completely happy at home, everything was great. Until that ugly head of abuse showed itself to me again.

My childhood sweetheart turned out to be a cheater and a mental abuser. When you are a teenager and you think you have everything figured out and life is all good.

I was broken hearted by what my boyfriend did to me. My parents were great to me and there was no reason for me to leave home, but sadly, I did. I left home because I was an emotional mess. My boyfriend cheating on me was the reason why I left with my oldest son Samuel, whose father I never loved. Does this make any sense? No, I was just a kid, searching for love.

I was only fifteen years old when I first experienced physical abuse. When it began and I just did not understand why this man treated me so cruelly! When I found out that I was pregnant with my son Samuel, this man thought my vitamins, given to me by my prenatal doctor, were to have an abortion. He threatened to burn my face with a steak fork. Not long after Samuel was born, I just couldn't take anymore and I realized that for the safety of my son and my own safety, I must get out of this bad relationship.

I went back home with my parents and I was happy to be back. I was safe now and that was all that mattered to me. Samuel's father could not hurt me anymore and I was not going to let him ever hurt me again.

My life was so much happier. I started dating my brother's buddy. My one night affair with my Brother Arturo's friend Grant is when Manuel was conceived.

Grant and I were great friends and even after he was born, we remained great friends. This man did not have an evil bone in his body. Manuel was not a planned pregnancy so Grant and I never got married nor did we live together, I always felt

Manuel was mine all alone. What a beautiful little boy. I guess this is why I named him Manuel all by myself. Not because I thought he was beautiful but because he was all mine. That's how it seemed to me and I was okay with that.

Through the years, we moved from home to home and apartment to apartment. We had a beautiful home on Mitchell Street and I thought we were happy. We relocated again to a home on Fifth Street in North Camden.

I was now nineteen with two babies out of wedlock. Samuel was in day care and my mother would care for Manuel so I could work at our neighborhood Burger King. Arturo and I were very close. I remember one afternoon we went to Philadelphia to see the movie "Thank God It's Friday", which Donna Summer appeared in. I will always have great memories of my brother Arturo.

My brother Arturo relocated to Wisconsin for a short time with our other brother, Lee. Oh how I missed Arturo dearly and I would write often to tell him how much he was missed. Arturo came back home and we were all so happy to have him back. Then it happened!

In the summer of 1980, a stray bullet that was meant for another person killed my brother Arturo. I'm sure you realize that I did not take my brother's death very well and it took me years to accept... One of my brother's famous sayings was, "Never go down to their level because you are better then all of them." I will always cherish the memories of my wonderful brother Arturo John Ortiz.

My sister Edwina separated from her husband of 10 years and she too became addicted to heroin. "Why?" I often asked myself, "Why?" Edwina loved her family and she was a good mother, wife and daughter. This terrible drug destroyed so many lives, including my brothers Lee and Ralph, as well as my sister Edwina.

At the time of my brother's death, I was now dating an old friend from the neighborhood. Until this very day, I can't figure out why I continued to look for the special person in my life. What was the reason? I kept looking for a decent man and I could never find him, I dated Troy for about a year and it was kind of rocky because we both had our 'extra' relationships. Who am I kidding; we cheated on one another.

During our rocky relationship, I became pregnant with my daughter Elizabeth. I always knew that Troy did not want to be with me during my pregnancy. Troy's niece and I had an altercation and the next thing I knew we were both rolling on the ground physically fighting while I was seven months pregnant.

A woman knows in her heart that the man in her life is supposed to protect her and be there for her. Sadly, I just couldn't find that man. Elizabeth was only a year old when Troy and I parted ways. Troy was a controlling, selfish dictator and I couldn't take it anymore, so we parted ways.

The relationship became abusive so I left; I knew it was the best thing to do. I didn't sit around and wait to see what was going to happen next.

During the time that I was with Troy, I met Taylor. Yes, I was living with Troy and I have no regrets about meeting Taylor.

I realized that I was unable to afford my apartment and now I had three children to take care of so I went to live with my sister Marcia. Taylor R. Levin, "Wow!" When I think of him now and how kind he was, I know I was not what he wanted. I was a single mother with three children, not one but three. Even in today's society, no man wants a woman with three children.

We were both young and Taylor was not ready for a family. He showed no signs of abusive behavior so it was nice to be with him. I will always remember Taylor as a loving man and I feel blessed to have met him.

San Juan, Puerto Rico

II

The day I met my 'Knight in shining armor' will live with me for the rest of my life. It was in January of 1983. I always felt it was love at first sight.

My mother was visiting and taking care of my father's mother in Puerto Rico. I know this is where I get my love and compassion for other people. My grandmother, as I said before, was not so kind to Mami or to us. As my brother's, sister's, and I became adults, we often discussed how much we missed the experience of having a grandmother.

My mother always believed in helping those that needed her help. She went to Puerto Rico to help my father's mother who had abandoned him. I took my son Samuel to visit my father to see if he needed anything to be done for him like cooking or cleaning, but Papi said he was just fine.

Papi drove us back to my sister's apartment. At times, I am able to laugh about this, but the women in our family speak very strongly and some people would say we were a tad bit loud, but I didn't think so.

Papi and I were coming into the apartment and that is when I saw Mark.

My heart skipped a beat I and I thought to myself, "Wow what a hunk!" Mark was a very handsome, tall man with a bronze complexion. To look at him, any woman would melt. His voice was soft and calm as he spoke.

Mark and my sister Marcia had been old hangout buddies since the disco-era. They had remained good friends ever since.

Okay, so I found this man extremely attractive. My knees were weak and I thought I would play it cool even though, I will admit, I found it difficult to catch my breath. I did realize that I had caught Mark's eye. I found him to be staring at me and we would lock eyes. As I walked into my sister's bedroom to call my nephew Jake, I couldn't but help to overhear the conversation, which was taking place in the living room. My heart was beating a mile a minute.

Mark was having a conversation with our next-door neighbor Sonia who asked him what he did for a living. Mark the proud man that he is, said he was a Philadelphia Police Officer. Now, the next words that came out of Sonia's mouth were not what anyone or I would have expected. Her comment should have helped me.

Sonia made it quite clear to Mark that she would never date a cop. Mark was offended as he told me later on in one of our conversations. He said, "Like I was interested in her ...ha, ha, ha, ha, ha."

Sometimes I laugh when I think about how young and silly Mark and I were. We would make goo-goo eyes at one another while I would stand in the door way of the kitchen while we kept looking at one another. My sister told me what a great guy he was and she said that I should talk to him. I thought, "Why not?" Taylor and I were just bed buddies and it was quite obvious that our relationship was not going to go any further. So, I decided to talk to Mark. We started chatting on the sofa and I could tell he didn't want to leave so I made the suggestion that we go to the liquor store to get a bottle of wine.

Mark agreed and we decided to go to the liquor store. The entire time that I was standing waiting to buy the bottle, Mark was standing right behind me. Back then, I was a considered to be a 'looker' in some men's eyes; Mark complimented me. I could feel his eyes on my back and how I felt like a school girl.

We got back to my sister's place and Mark and I were both seated on the sofa as we had a glass of wine and just talked. We talked about his family and he showed me a picture of his little brother Michael, which I thought was so cute. Mark was still a young rookie on the job and I am sure he never dreamed of having children at his young age I was twenty-two years old and Mark was twenty-three. I was a young single mother with three children out of wedlock. Mark didn't have any children of his own.

We both realized that it was getting late and Mark's friend Robert wanted to leave. I do remember he wasn't too happy that Mark was talking to me. Maybe he felt that I wasn't good enough for Mark; I guess I will never know.

As I walked Mark to the door, he tried to give me our first kiss on the lips. I turned my head and the kiss landed on my cheek. I thought, "Hey, big guy, not so fast"! Nevertheless, it was sweet. I remember how we laughed later on about it. He would say later, "It's not like you never had been kissed before or even had sex before." My response to Mr. Wonderful was, "Hey it doesn't matter, this is who I am."

I gave Mark my phone number and truthfully, I never thought he would call. Even Sonia didn't believe Mark would call so I just shrugged it off. It really didn't matter all that much.

The following morning to my surprise, I received a phone call from Mark. I was so surprised and quite pleased that maybe he did like me. I personally thought we hit it off pretty good.

During our phone conversation Mark told me that he had enlisted in the Navy and he was taking military leave from the police department, I thought it was a great thing to do. I realized then that he was just going to be someone I was going to date for the time being and I understood.

We met on a Thursday evening and the following Friday went on a date. There was a nightclub in the 4th district at a hotel. Until this day, I remember exactly what I was wearing. It was a white top with feathers around the neck and brown pants with black flat shoes. We sat and talked and it was obvious that I like to talk. So I talked and talked, and he just listened. I don't even think we danced that evening. We decided to leave and we ran into some of his buddies from the police department. I realize now that most cops back then would like to hang around the night club to see the young ladies instead of patrolling the neighborhood.

This was when Mark and I really had our first kiss in his red little car in front of his co-workers. I personally felt he wanted to show-off and I thought it was just a perfect kiss. We drove back to my sister's apartment and we sat on the sofa and did a bit more hugging and kissing. Mark was always a gentleman and it was nice to have someone treat me like a lady and NOT a pin cushion.

From the moment, we met Mark and I tried to spend as much time with one another as possible. He was leaving on my 23rd birthday and I knew this relationship was not going to last forever. I just felt lucky to have someone.

I always felt when people come into your life you cherish as much time with them as possible because you never know what the outcome may be.

One early morning around 2:00am, Mark and I were holding each other just talking after making love. I knew that making love with him was all right. I had nothing to lose because I already had three children and he was leaving for the Navy. I felt some sadness in heart. Mark was also sad too. We just started to get to know one another and he had to leave. He made comments of how he made a mistake to have enlisted into the service and I would say don't feel that way. It's great you have decided to join the Navy.

Then out of nowhere, Mark asked me to marry him. I was stunned! Mark was the first man who ever asked me to marry him. I had three children and not one of those wonderful men of course I am being sarcastic asked me to marry them. I made it quite clear to Mark that this was not a joking matter and this was quite serious not to joke around about such a sensitive situation. Mark said, "He was quite serious."

I would be a liar if I did not admit this: why would this man want to marry me? I was a single mother, poor with little education. Why? I fell in love with this man because it did not matter to him that I had three children and I was poor.

I am proud of myself. I did my very best with what I had. Yes! I was on welfare and I depended on the system. God, there were times I would not eat so my children could. I always felt good about myself until....

The next morning I told my sister, Marcia that Mark had proposed to me. We were both shocked and I was still trying to take it all in even to the point that I still questioned why? Why did this man want to marry a woman with three children? Mark had no children. He had a great career and he was getting ready to go overseas so why?

The first family member that I met was his sister Delia. During our entire conversation, I kept thinking "wow! She is really great and beautiful." My future sister in law Delia was a fair-skinned African American woman with light hair, green eyes and a tiny perfect body.

Delia's gift was her gift of gab. Later on, I realized she could talk her way out of anything. Well, almost anything. Later on in my marriage, I came to realize my sister-in-law reason to become close to me was for selfish reasons. At the time of my engagement to Mark, Delia had left her husband to date another man and she wanted her mother's approval.

Henry was located in California and she was jetting back and forth. I always knew that family members were very protective of one another but....this family has a complete different story behind them.

Then, I met my mother in law Doris. I thought the moment I met her that she looked so much like Lena Horn and how beautiful she was and I came to realize that beauty was only on the outside because the inside was nothing but a fake, a lie. My future mother in law attended church every Sunday. I was judge, criticized, and crucified from day one!

I watched as Doris went into her closet and pulled out Mark's old report cards. Even until this very day I truly did not understand what the purpose of her showing me his old report cards; did she judge and felt that all Latinos were ignorant, was it because my parents did not speak English did she feel they were stupid? What was taught to her as a young woman?

Doris was kind enough to show me the family tree documents and the history of her family. Doris next breath was to say to me was, I would have to read the newspaper more and listen to classical music, I was a bit shocked and offended. My future mother in law would speak to me if I was an idiot. I guess in her eyes that most Latina women were ignorant. I never dreamed in a hundred years how difficult it was going to be as time went on.

I learned to watch, listen and absorbed the behavior of this family.

Mark's grandmother would tell her stories and I felt like a sponge as I absorbed everything she told to me. However, there was truly something wrong with this family.

Mark's great, great, great grandfather was the Governor of North Carolina who owned slaves. A bi-racial family raised his great, great grandmother. I later discovered that Mark's great, great grandmother was the child of an unwed mother. All those years she thought, she was from a bi-racial mother and father when in fact she was Caucasian. Mark's great, great grandfather was an Episcopalian priest. He also had a dark secret in that his first marriage there was a son who died at birth. Both mother and son died of syphilis. Mark's great, great grandfather was a very abusive man. He abused his wife, daughters and son.

Many African Americans who were of very fair complexion would deny their race. Many members of

Marks' family would also say that they are not African American.

Mark had a great uncle who served in the military. He never told his commanders that he was African American and when they found out, they sent him to the segregated barracks. The reception he was given was not pleasant or welcoming. He had also not told his fiancé of his heritage and she in turn, broke off the engagement. Mark's great grandmother told me that his great uncle had committed suicide in her home. I realized then that this family had issues and they were not as perfect as they portrayed themselves to be.

So, this gave the grandmother the right to turn her nose down on every race including her own. You were not accepted if you spoke a different language, you were not accepted, if your skin was a different color. Even before we said, "I do", I was doomed! I experienced nothing but negativity from this family. My ex use to say I was negative but he never understood it was because of him and his family. I was once a positive person but I married into a horrible family. I allowed myself to feel unworthy

When I met Mark's grandmother Margo, I thought, "Oh, wow, this woman is quite a 'pickle'" I am being very polite when I say 'pickle'. Margo thought I was pretty, but too tall. The head of the family was not a very polite woman. I thought to myself, "'Oh I guess I am going to have to cut off my legs." The family did not approve of me. I was poor and I was a Puerto Rican woman with three children. I was not good enough for their son, brother and grandson.

As far as Mark's family was concerned, I had nothing going for myself. I was light skinned, with good hair but they did not want any dark skinned women in their family.

I never dreamed I would go through so much heartache and sadness. I prayed so often for love and support. I dreamed that maybe one day they would love me and accept me for me but it never happened!

One particular afternoon as Mark and I were leaving Mark's Mother Doris' apartment, I met his other grandmother, Angel. At first, my gut told me Angel wouldn't like me but I was so wrong. I thought because Mark's grandmother and mother did not care for me, the rest of the family would feel the same way.

My visit with his other family members was not what I had hoped it would be. I just knew Angel was going to judge me the same way Doris and Margo had judged me. I felt very defensive and standoffish.

I thought Mark's father would feel the same way as well. I was wrong about Angel; that's right she became my angel. The love I felt for her was the way I should have felt for my mother-in-law but I never did have a positive relationship with Mark's mother.

I never thought that my father-in-law disliked me, but we will save that for later.

It makes to sad to think of this, but even my Papi questioned why Mark would want to marry me. Papi, wanted to know why didn't Mark want to marry my sister Marcia, since she was single with no children.

Papi felt that my sister was the perfect woman Mark needed. I would be a liar if I did not say this really hurt

my feelings but I could not express this to Pop. For all these years, I kept the sadness in my heart. For so many years, I felt I was not worthy and I stood by, year after year, allowing men to treat me poorly. You know, I often felt that my father had a valid point.

My brother Ralph felt our marriage was bound to fail too. He said we were not from the same neighborhood and mark was a police officer. I was an unwed mother with three children and I had nothing. From the very beginning of our marriage, there was negativity and this continued with us for years into our married life.

During the snowstorm of 1983, Mark was not able to drive to New Jersey to see me. Valentine's Day is a day that will always be a memory of a romantic day for me. Mark was going to be leaving very soon to boot camp.

As the date came closer for Mark to leave, sadness began to take over. I tried to stay positive because I wanted to be strong for Mark.

On February 14, 1983, Mark R. Stuns proposed to me and it was the happiest day of my life. I couldn't believe my dream was coming true. I had met a wonderful man who loved me for me and loved my three beautiful children. I was surely blessed and I was so overcome with joy and happiness. I felt like I could go to the highest mountain and just scream; I wanted to thank God for this wonderful man.

This was such a happy day for me that I shared my joy with my sister Sonia as I showed her my ring. It was not a large stone, but it was the largest stone to me.

On February 26, 1983, my finance left for Great Lakes, IL and to see him leave just broke my heart. I needed to be strong because I hoped and prayed that he would come back to me and we would be married.

Mark asked his mother to keep in touch with me during his time in boot camp, but of course, you know Doris didn't. Poor Mark thought his mother and sister would continue to have a relationship with me but it never happened. I made sure I sent Mark positive letters during his time in the military. No matter how lonely and sad I felt, I knew that my future mother-in-law would never accept me.

The women in Mark's life had a very big influence on him and his grandfather had died several years earlier of cancer. This was before I ever met Mark. Mark said, "I wish you could have met him, he would have loved to meet you and the kids." I am so sorry that I never got the chance to meet this sweet man. Maybe if he was alive they would have never had interfered in our marriage.

Weeks went by and I received my first letter from Mark. Oh, how I missed him. I kept my letters always sounding happy because I wanted him to think that everything was just great. I never let on that his family did not communicate with me.
I received two wonderful love letters and the first was written like this:

March 10, 1983
8:00 PM

Dear Carmen,

It's freezing up here. There's snow all over the ground and its 20 degrees, but last week it was 70 degrees. Big change! I was dreaming about you last night. We were embraced, and you said you would wait for me. I hope it's still true. (I won't tell you about the sexy dreams I have about you). I'm always thinking about you. They're going to let us have a few pictures now, so I told my mom in a letter to send the pictures of us. Were learning

Rosaura Torres

how to drill with rifles right now, I look pretty sharp, naturally.

I just got your letters. Thanks a lot; it was good to hear from you. The letters smelled good and remind me of you. I love you so much you just can't imagine. I wish I never joined this outfit. If I had one wish, I'd be home right now. This place can be worse than prison sometimes.

As for your modeling career, there are many things you must consider. Modeling is a fast-paced industry surrounded by a world of drugs, disappointment and sexual favors. It's tough to make it and you can hardly trust anybody, especially if you don't know them. You're very pretty just like I always said and I don't doubt you could make it.

Delia was a model for about a year and she could really answer all the questions you want to ask. Please remember most guys who tell you they want to photograph you are usually just telling you a "line" to get in your pants. A lot of them slip something in your drink when you're not looking. If you want to do it, you have my blessing, because I would never stop you from doing something. But let Delia guide you, call her and ask her about it. She can tell you some good things and some bad things about modeling. Remember it's time consuming, but if you get in shape and take care of your health, I know you can handle it. The final decision has to be yours, but thanks for letting me know. I would never want to see you get hurt, like I am now. When I joined the Navy, I did it without thinking about anything else and now I am regretting it. If some of the guys here weren't so nice, I would have lost my mind by now. I miss you so much I just can't explain.

I love you forever

Mark

Second letter from Mark

March 13, 1983
9:30 PM

Dear Carmen,
It's Sunday and we have a few hours to ourselves, but we still have to stay in our barracks. It really sucks. This has got to be the worst mistake I ever made. I miss you

and home so much. Soon we might be able to make a phone call, if we do it will probably only be for 5 minutes. The name of this base is "Great Lakes"; most of us call it "Great Mistake". When I joined I was bored and lonely, I thought this would add excitement to my life. I never dreamed I could meet someone like you. You're the best thing that ever happened to me, If I can find a legal way to get out of here I will. You never appreciate some of the things you have in life until they are taken away from you. We were to graduate Friday April 22nd. We don't know if we'll go on leave or not. Like everything else here "it depends". We will definitely get free time that weekend but we might have to be back at mid nite, or if we're lucky 6:30 am the next day. Either way it sucks. I'll try to get you to California, and maybe Memphis, or Florida. A lot of things can change in the Navy, just like my time got cut down from 47 weeks to 32 weeks. Hopefully they will cut it down some more, or maybe I'll get a change in orders. Either way you look at it I wish I was the fuck back home. If I had no one to care for, or had someone to care for me like you do, I could probably handle this, but I love you more than anyone or anything in life, please never forget that.

Love, Mark

P.S. I LOVE YOU

When you're young, you want to believe that love can last forever and that special man you allowed into your life would never hurt or cause you any pain. In all my life, I never dreamed that my love for Mark would be so wonderful.

I am so thankful to my sister for allowing us to live with her, I had nowhere to go and she took us in. My sister and I were not getting along because she had a two bedroom apartment that was quite small. I understand it was quite difficult for her. It was getting pretty cramped in the small apartment so it was quite frustrating. You know when you're young you never truly express yourself the way as you get older. I was quite grateful to her though.

One afternoon I received a phone call from Mark and I became so emotional that I started to cry. He said, "I wanted to surprise you but you spoiled the surprise I have to tell you, I am coming home." I couldn't believe my ears; the Navy could not give him the school that he signed up for so they offered him another school or an honorable discharge. Mark took the honorable discharged and a month after he had left, he returned home.

I called Doris to see if it was possible for me to come along to the airport to see Mark when he arrived home. Doris didn't feel it was a good idea for me to go along. The truth is that Doris didn't want Mark back home because she was hoping that he would stay in the military, forget about me, and eventually call off the engagement.

Mark told me that when he got home he wanted to come to see me right away but Doris became very upset. Mark thought that his mother just missed him a lot, but he couldn't see that she just didn't approve of me, or he was too blind to see it.

I was so happy to finally see Mark. He had that silly military buzz cut and was very thin but I thought he looked great; how happy we were to be with one another again. In April of 1983, Mark moved the children and me to Philadelphia, PA. We lived right around the corner from his grandmother's house at 3200 King Avenue. It was a three-floor house with a very small kitchen. We were renting this precious home at the time. How I want to scream, this is where my nightmare began.

Our wedding date was scheduled for June 25, 1983. I was so overwhelmed with trying to prepare for this wedding. Mark arrived back from the Navy in April and we were rushing for a wedding in June. I don't know why such the rush but we did rush; my head felt like it was going to spin off.

My future mother-in-law offered to help with the expenses towards the wedding and Mark's grandmother's friend, Ms. Dee, made my wedding dress. So, let me be short and to the point, my future mother-in-law made all the wedding arrangements, from the flowers to the church. That was because my church would not marry us unless Mark converted to Catholicism; he refused.

Mark's grandmother was very happy to hear that we were getting married at St. James Episcopal Church at 32nd and Pine. I wanted my family to be a bigger part of my wedding plans but because they weren't, Mark felt they didn't have any right to complain about anything.

This is when the controlling started taking place and I would not say a word. The only thing I really picked out was my wedding dress and my bridesmaid dresses. I even wore my sister-in-law's wedding vale. Please do not mistake me; I was very grateful. I just wanted my family to be a bigger part of what was supposed to be the best thing in my life, other than giving birth to my children.

I first asked Marcia to be my maid of honor but that didn't work out as I had hoped and prayed so Wendy Sanchez became my maid of honor. Wendy arranged my bridal shower and it didn't turn out exactly as I hoped either. So, because of that, my future mother-in-law arranged a bridal shower at Mark's grandmother's house. I thought that was very nice of her but damn, I just never understood why at one minute she was kind and the next minute she could be so cold and cruel.

Deep down inside I thought, "Maybe I have a chance with her, maybe she will love me and my children." They were little guys and my baby Elizabeth was so young. Samuel was 6, Manuel was 4 and Elizabeth was 1 ½ years old. When Mark and I were married, my little guys were so excited because they were going to have a Pop, and not just Elizabeth, because from time to time, her father was still in her life.

When I think how horrible my mother-in-law and Mark's grandmother treated my boys I just wanted to scream.

44

My poor babies, they just wanted to be loved like I did and it didn't turn out the way I prayed it would.
I decided to spend my last night as a single woman with my mother and father. I was so nervous; I felt like a little girl. We even slept in the same bed and Mami and I talked until three in the morning. What I would give to have that moment again with my mother and father.

Mark decided before the wedding that he wanted to adopt my boys. Troy, Elizabeth's father, would not allow it even though Mark was a good father to her. I kept saying, "He must really love my son's." What man would just outright take on the responsibility of another man's children? The only reason Mark adopted them was because he did not want to deal with their biological father's. I realized this much later on in our marriage and my son's felt exactly the same way I did. I should have spoken up; why didn't I say something? My sons suffered by the hands of this family and the memory of the verbal and physical abuse will live with them always. I just let them walk all over me and my children.

In my heart, I always questioned if Mark's love was real and true or if he really loved us at all. I don't think my question will ever be answered.

My wedding was on June 25, 1983 and it was a perfect summer day that I will always remember. Several of my friends as well as my maid of honor came to my mother's house. They were taking pictures and the one thing that was missing was my vale. Everyone commented on how unusual I looked because I did not have my vale. I called Mark in the morning to see if it was possible for my dad and Sister Edwin to pick up my vale. We argued over it, but I always felt that with patience and understanding we would be okay. Anyway, my father and sister were able to pick up my veil. Oh! Let me correct myself, it was my ex-sister-in-law's veil.

The limo picked us up, a little behind schedule, and I was so nervous. My girl Darlene noticed how nervous I was and how rigid I was sitting; I was a nervous wreck. They were able to sneak in some wine, which I drank to calm down a little. Well low and behold, the priest wanted to speak to me and I thought, "Oh darn, my breath must smell of wine". I always felt like our priest did not care too much for me. I thought I was being a bit paranoid and I ignored it. Years later, my priest committed suicide and jumped off the Strawberry Mansion Bridge. Maybe it was a message from God trying to tell me something; I will never know. I often think of him and pray that he is at peace.

Mark later confessed to me how nervous he was on our wedding day because he thought I was going to back out of the wedding. I wondered until this very day why this would even cross his mind. Mark was my dream, but I held on to the memory of Tony because I often wondered if Mark truly loved me.

As Papi and I waited to walk down the aisle, I watched my little man Samuel walk with the pillow in his hand. I watched and thanked God for this perfectly wonderful day and I thanked him for my handsome little guy, Samuel.

The time had come for my father and me to walk slowly down the aisle. I tried so carefully to walk down the aisle without any difficulties. My knees were shaking and I continued to take step after step. Just when I thought I had made it, I accidently tripped on the front of my gown. I hoped that no one would notice, but unfortunately, Mark's grandmother did and of course, she commented on the fact that I tripped. Hey, it happens. I looked straight ahead and I saw the handsome, soon to be, husband of mine. I could not believe that I was going to be someone's wife. Me!

Someone loved me and wanted me for the rest of their life.

Mark and I faced the priest and as he continued forward with our vows everything was going perfectly until the priest said, "If anyone can find cause why these two people should not be wed, speak now or forever hold your peace."

As I looked up at our priest, he just kept looking around waiting for someone to disapprove of our marriage; I could not believe my eyes and ears. Why do they ask this question? I felt doomed from the beginning. Maybe this marriage was never meant to be.

Rosaura Torres

In my silly ways, I tried to convince myself that Mark's mother and grandmother had the priest do this but I know they would not embarrass Mark like that. Maybe I am wrong, but this and so many other questions in my life I will never be able to answer to.

Later on in my marriage and I viewed my wedding album it was obvious how sad Doris and Margo were on our wedding day; it even made me sad.

We had a wonderful Honeymoon. The Poconos were just beautiful; I took a picture of Mark petting a lamb. I could never understand why he kept having this funny smile on his face but later on he explained to me that we were like two little kids running up and down the halls, or horseback riding; we were just trying to get to know one another. I remember the big Hershey Kiss that was waiting for us when we got into our room. We were both thin and we could afford to eat a big Hershey Kiss; it was fun.

The Honeymoon couldn't last forever and we returned home. Then things started going so wrong. Delia was supposed to be babysitting my little ones and so was my mother-in-law, but Delia was busy playing house with Robert. Yes, Robert that introduced us. Poor Samuel told me that he was the one babysitting everyone because Delia was busy on the third floor with Robert.

I was furious with Delia but sadly, I was not allowed to make waves so I kept my mouth shut and had to go with the program. I allowed Mark to take control of everything in my life, even my way of thinking and how I dressed. I changed the way I looked to please him. He wanted me to dress like a preppie. Some of my old friends thought I was into some sort of religion because of the way I was dressing. I was not the person I once was. I realized that even when I was struggling I was very happy with myself no matter how poor I was. I often wonder if he felt he did a great thing for society by marrying a Latina woman from the ghetto. I would rather, he never asked me, so I could be free from an abusive relationship, which felt like I had entered into an evil den.

I continued in a marriage that was abusive in every way.

Mark and I were newlyweds and my mother-in-law started making it a habit of showing up without calling. One early morning Mark and I were making love and she was knocking at the door. Mark said to ignore it but Doris would not go away so he had to open the door. I sat on the steps and Doris asked me the unbelievable question, she wanted to know why my face was so red. All I could do was look over at Mark and then I think she finally got it. Wow, she amazed me. This was just the beginning of the bullshit and I wonder now how I ever put up with it. How did I do it? How these three women in Mark's life could be so insensitive and so uncaring, I will never know. But wait, as time continued on I did my own analyzing.

One afternoon Marks' other grandmother, Angel, had invited the entire family to her home for dinner. At the dinner table in front of everyone, Margo corrected my English. I was so embarrassed I did not know where to hang my head in shame and then Angel came to my defense. From that moment on, our relationship grew more until we were more like daughter-in-law and mother-in-law; I really like her.

Angel and I would go shopping and eat dinner out together. We grew to be very close and I always confided in her. She knew of the abuse I endured by her grandson that I couldn't even tell my mother because I was so ashamed and embarrassed.

A part of my children's abuse started with emotional and verbal affects. One afternoon Margo picked the boys up from school and she made it quite clear to Samuel's teacher that Mark was not their father and that Mark adopted them. My little guy was so upset and this started some fighting. No matter how much I tried to be a part of this family, it was never going to work. I was not what they wanted and they made it quite clear how they felt. I didn't like that they subjected my boy's to their cruelty.

Mark loved his family and I know he could either not see what was going on, or was he just a wimp. I did voice my feelings, but he didn't listen to me.

One particular weekend the school was sponsoring a fair, which took place down the street from our home. Margo had invited us to go and I agreed; I thought it would be nice. Samuel ran into one of his classmates at the fair and Margo yelled at my son to get away from the nigger. I could not believe my ears when I heard the words that came out of her mouth.

The neighborhood was made up mostly of African Americans and here was this sad and bitter woman placing herself, as well as my children, and me in danger with her hateful and vile language. I was not raised to be a racist and I had no plan to raise my children in such a hateful environment. The woman was an embarrassment to us all. I made an excuse that the children were tired and as quickly as I could I left the park. I knew that the best thing to do was to leave.

Margo would never call herself an African American. What a very sad woman she was. She considered herself to be colored and if you were not light skinned you did not belong in her circle; she didn't hesitate to let it be known.

In time, I realized that this marriage was not going to work. I was married into a racist and bigoted family. The braining washing bullshit that was shoved into this man's head until this very day leaves me speechless!

This entire family was raised to believe that because they were light skinned they were better than any other race, even their own. They believed that if you are a dark skinned African American person you are useless. Time and time again, I would hear the hateful remarks about people of other nationalities.

Mark was raised in an elite organization that called themselves by the name "Jack and Jill". Margo told me the history of the organization and that no dark skinned blacks were allowed to join this club. Now, being Puerto Rican, I had no idea a club like this ever existed. The saying back then was you had to pass the "brown paper bag test"; if you failed, you could not be a member. Margo was one of the original members of Jack and Jill.

Racism and bigotry is hateful; my experience with the hatred of other races turned my stomach. Many people like Mark were raised with such vile teachings, it should never matter what color skin you have, and I was raised to believe that God loves us all.

One afternoon Mark and I went to look at some furniture that his Grandmother Margo's friend had put up for sale. As we drove around, out of nowhere, Mark's grandmother began to tell me the story how many of her afternoons were spent going to the movies with her friend. I just listened quietly and took everything in. You see, Grandmother Margo had an affair that lasted for 50 years. As the family would talk about it, I learned just how much this family was not so prim and proper after all.
Mark angrily told me Grandmother Margo's friend's name was Mr. Tubbs. He said that his mother was angry with her mother because Grandmother Margo wanted to leave her husband and go with Mr. Tubbs but she knew the best thing to do was to stay because of the kids. The marriage was not a happy one so Grandmother Margo continued her affair with Mr. Tubbs.

I only spoke of it with Mark, but the rest of the time, I quietly watched and listened.
Doris became extremely tired of my sister-in-law Delia's bullshit and kicked her out of her home. Delia ended up coming to live in our home. I was not working at the time and we were doing our best to make it on Mark's

income. He was bringing in only $18,000 a year and back then, that was not very much. Delia was not working and Mark was very upset because he was trying to provide for a wife and three children as well. I was not allowed to say anything. My mother-in-law made it quite clear that I had no right to an opinion because I was not employed. Therefore, again as usual, the silence took over and the tension continued to grow as time went on. I wanted my marriage and I wanted more than anything for Mark and me to get to know each other better. How could we though when his family continued to do everything in their power to interfere in the business of our marriage and our family.

During the time Delia was living with us, we had Marks' younger sister Monica from his Dad come to visit. Mark's cousin Leroy came over for dinner too. Everyone was eating, drinking, and having a good time until Delia had too much to drink. That is when Delia started telling Monica about how her mother had broke up her mother and fathers' marriage.

You see, it turned out that Monica's mother Jezebel was having an affair with my father-in-law Jordon while he was married to Doris. It got to the point where Doris had piled up Mark and Delia in the car and followed Jordon to Jezebels' apartment.
All hell broke loose at dinner. Monica said it was a lie and Delia said, "No it's the truth." Monica called her father and then things got even worse. Mark confirmed it with Monica. My father-in-law was very angry with Mark because he felt that as the sensible one, Mark should not have allowed this to happen. For almost two years, Mark did not speak to his father because of this. In some ways, I felt sorry for Delia.

Delia resented Jezebel for taking her father away. My father-in-law did not raise Mark and Delia. Mark was just happy that he was lucky enough to have his grandfather in his life. His father was not a big part of his life and this didn't seem to matter to him that much. I believe poor Delia was affected by her father's leaving and I believed that was the reason her life was such a mess.

Finally, Delia's welcome was wearing out. One afternoon, my mother-in-law came storming into the house and to my surprise, she started yelling at Delia. I just sat there numb and I could not believe how this woman was disrespecting my home. She dared to come into my home and just act as if I didn't exist!

Next, crazy woman turned and became angry with me. I now became her target and she wanted to know what my problem was, I said, "Oh, nothing, I am just sitting here." I had to call Mark. You would think that with all the nonsense, Delia would have left; but she continued to live with us.

I finally concluded that I was done for. If I made a comment, I was wrong. If I kept my comments to myself, I was wrong. All of this struggling to keep my thoughts and feelings to myself was making me ill.

When I looked at Mark, I tried to see a strong, positive man, but in reality, he was not so strong. All this arguing and the cruel behavior from Margo and my mother-in-law were going to affect the children and me; it seemed like he really didn't care. I will never know how he really felt.

One evening Uncle Ed and Aunt Lucy were visiting and no one called Mark to tell him. Uncle Ed had come from NY and Aunt Macy came from Boston. When I saw the look of sadness on Mark's face, I felt his pain and I guess this is when he realized that the reason they did not call him was that they did not want the children or I over for dinner. Mark walked around the corner and had a drink with them and we were left at home. I sat there feeling like he was clueless and I was doomed. I was in hell and I was dying inside. With every blow of disrespect and humiliation I received from this family, my spirit was fighting to stay alive.

Delia was still living with us and still dating Robert. One afternoon Delia was expecting a phone call from Robert. My friend from Camden had called and I asked Robert if he could give me five minutes and call back. I did tell Delia that Robert called and he was going to call back but this didn't matter to her. She became infuriated, grabbed me by the arms, and dug her fake nails into me. My reflexes took over and my arms pulled back; I punch her dead in the face!

Dick, who was our best man of our wedding, was visiting and he grabbed me and I pulled away and I went into my bedroom. All they kept saying was "wait until Mark get's home." Mark arrived home and came into the bedroom to talk to me. I thought it was going to go smoothly but I was wrong. I was sitting on the floor listening to music, Mark walked into the bedroom, and he started yelling at me, he wanted to know if the ghetto in me was coming out. I said, "It has nothing to do with me being from the ghetto, it has to do with respect." That is when it got physical. Mark kicked me while I was on the ground and grabbed me up off the floor. I could not believe what just happened; he knew he had promised me he would never put his hands on me again, but he did!

Things were never the same after that incident. Delia knew that she could say and do whatever pleased her. I never dreamed the man I loved and married would hit me.

I confided in him about my experiences in the past and I just wanted him to love and respect me. When Mark hit me for the first time, I knew this was going to be just the beginning of a lot of pain.

Mark promised me that he would never hit me again. In November of 1983, I became very ill. I developed a cyst on my ovaries and they had to operate. Margo was very

58

angry because she wanted more great grandchildren and I had my tubes tied two years before I married Mark. Truthfully, we could have had children but it worked out for the best that we never did. During my illness, Grandmother Margo was upset because I became ill and she insisted that Mark still attend Thanksgiving dinner in Washington, DC. She wanted him to leave me in the hospital. I could he see what his mother, sister and grandmother were doing but apparently, he could not.

Things didn't work out for Delia and Robert and at times, she dated other men. One was a singer who made sure she led the lifestyle that her family convinced her she should. Delia always thought she deserved the best of everything. I once met a news anchor from Philly that she was dating; he was a completely different story. We were at a Philly nightclub that was located at the Marriot Hotel. The news anchor and I will call him Mr. Haines; he would probably not remember this because he was so intoxicated. The next words that came out of this man's mouth completely knocked me for a loop.

Mr. Haines asked me what made me Puerto Rican. Now I had a blank look on my face because I could have said, "Hey shithead, my mother and father", but I thought, let me be a lady, and before I could answer him he said, "I bet you never spent one day in Puerto Rico." I said, "No I have not, I was born in Milwaukee, Wisconsin." Mr. Haines looked like he already had been drinking when he looked at my dress and he said, "I bet all you Puerto Rican women like wearing dresses like that, WOW!"

I knew after this unpleasant conversation with Mr. Haines that it was time to go. It took every ounce of my being not to curse this man out right there. I had one drink too many and I asked Delia if we could please go home. She was kind enough to agree because even Delia did not appreciate how he spoke to me. This was one time during my marriage to Mark I truly thought my sister-in-law actually liked me.

That following week Mr. Haines was invited to have dinner with us, but I made it quite clear that under any circumstances was this man coming into my home. We left it just as I wished. The following week I happen to be telling Mark's grandmother the story about Mr. Haines, her next comment left me gasping for air, "Well you know your race is known to be the low lives of all low lives". I could not believe my years and my husband was right there the entire time this sad, pathetic woman made that comment. Mark may have said something in response to the comment she made against my race, but you could barely make it out. Oh God, every fiber of my skinned crawled and I was completely disgusted. I have long since forgiven Mark's grandmother. God gave me enough love to remove the anger I felt.

My husband had enough of his sister Delia and he wanted her to move out of our home. My mother-in-law became angry with Mark and I and I could not understand why. Maybe my mother-in-law knew that somehow having Delia in our home would help destroy our marriage. What amazes me is that she was the one that threw her out of her place. I made up my mind that this woman had it out for me and my children and I knew things were going to get worse. Was I kidding myself trying to believe they would find some compassion in their hearts and respect for my babies and me? My marriage was a lie and this family was going to be the end of my being.

There have been so many times that I would sit and ponder and think, how much more can you take. What is it going to cost you? I never dreamed that it was going to cost me as much as it did.

Rosaura Torres

After my mother-in-law made that comment that, I had no right to say what went on in the household, I decided to look for work and I started part time at the Dental School at the University Of Pennsylvania. It was not as much as I wished that I had, so whatever amount I brought home I gave my entire paycheck to Mark to help with the bills.

One evening after work, I started examining my baby's eyes, I noticed this white shadow in her eye, and that is when I knew it; my daughter Elizabeth inherited cataracts from me. My baby was only two years old; all I could do was cry. The next morning, Mark and I went to see a doctor at Eye Hospital and I was right. My little girls' first eye surgery was performed when she was only two years old. Elizabeth was even the poster child for the Eye Hospital.

Elizabeth only had to say two words "Please help". I was so proud of my little girl and saddened by the problem with her eyes, I prayed to God that neither of my children would ever have to go through what I went through. Elizabeth and I appeared on the Today Show and we explained to the host about the eye problem that, Elizabeth and I had and the doctor who performed my eye surgery on me many years before, he also performed Elizabeth's eye surgery. During the time of my cataract surgery, it was not as advanced as it is today.

I continue to take on temp jobs to help Mark and the house hold as much as possible because I promised myself that I was not going to allow anyone ever again to say to me that, I was not allowed to voice my thoughts in my own home. I should have stood my ground and maybe I would have received the respect that I deserved.

I thought, giving so much of myself I would have gotten more respect from Mark's family. I gave my power; I gave up my control over my life. Mami and Papi even tried to speak with us but Mark felt that no one was going to tell him how to run his marriage so; they kept out of our marriage. And I continued with the silence of pain.

When Mark first put his hands on me, something inside died and more than anything, I wanted my marriage to work. I wanted my marriage but the dark hole that I had crawled into from the pain was so overwhelming.

I even signed over all my paychecks to Mark, I felt it was not enough, what I gave towards the household was never going to be enough.

I started working for Reliance Insurance Company and this is when Mark felt with both our incomes, it would be a great time to start looking for our own home. I was so happy and I knew it was time for us to have a home of our own.

My mother-in-law wanted Mark to find a house in their neighborhood. Mark felt that it would be better if the kids went to a school with children that were more diverse. You see after the incident in the park when my son Samuel was chased home from school, Mark stated that he just wanted the boys to be safe.

Now, what can I say about my father-in-law Jordon. He did not get into our affairs; my mother-in-law and Mark's grandmother and sister did more than their share of interference. My father-in-law had his own share of drama; my brother-in-law Bud was a handful. My memory of Bud's behavior goes back to one evening when Mark was called because Bud vandalized a movie theater and shredded the theater screen. The damage to the screen was over $10,000.

It was like my father-in-law had Bud and my mother-in-law had Delia. Mark's stepmother Jezebel pretended she never knew Mark's dad was a cheater; he was a player.

I guess everyone has someone that brings a lot of drama into your life. This family did time and time again, and all I could do was try to love them the best way I knew how.

We moved into our new home and I remember not long after we moved Doris made a comment that I took her son away from her. Wow, what was with this woman? Did she realize how much it meant to me to be a part of her family; that Mark would always be her son? Why couldn't the woman who had such a strong belief in God just give me the opportunity to be a part of her family? I loved her son.

No matter what I tried, I could not do enough. Doris was a hypocrite. You cannot go to church every Sunday, sing on the choir and act holier than thou and then turn around and treat small children as if they were nothing. In our wedding vowels it say's forsaking all others. Doris, Margo and Delia were supposed to give our marriage a chance instead of bringing constant drama and sorrow into our lives.

One evening not long before Mark and I relocated, Doris dropped by the house at King Avenue and I did not like the way she was talking to the children. I made myself very clear to her and I said, "If you ever hurt my children I will attack you like a lion attacks a human when they are trying to hurt their cubs". Doris said, "Do you believe I would hurt your children?" I said, "YES!"

Our new home was located at 200 West Ark Road, in the Olney section and I thought it was the greatest house ever. It had three bedrooms, two and a half baths and a finished basement. I was so happy to have our own home and I was still in a dark hole I did not realize why my heart was still so heavy.

Mark was the love of my life and not in a hundred years would I have dreamed he would ever put his hands on me. I continued through the motions and then I met Bart. The affair did not even last a month. There is no excuse for what I did and the sadness that I caused Mark was terrible. I felt guilty for what I did, but I was angry; angry at the man who I thought would never hurt me in a million years.

Yes, I was hit again and so were the walls. I was wrong for having this affair and I will always take full responsibility for it. Star, Mark's cousin was angry with me. Mark was angry at everyone because they all felt he was an idiot for staying. Why didn't he just leave me? I even felt he should have left; the best thing for Mark to do was to leave. We stayed in the marriage and further and further, I sunk into a deep, dark hole. I never understood why I felt the need to find someone that truly loved me.

The love and respect I have for Mark's cousin will always have a huge part of my heart until this very day. I will continue to love and respect her very much. The great times Star and I shared and the memories of hanging out, attending a music concert, or how we could laugh at the most simplest things. We could be so sad and in just a brief moment, a word or a look and the laughter would begin.

Star is a wonderful, awesome person and Mark and I tried everything we could to help her. Now, Uncle Ed was this big shot attorney for an insurance company and he refused

to send his daughter any money while Star was living with us so again here was Mark and I trying to do the best we could for another family member.

In such a short time of my life, I was truly amazed how I continued to meet unusual people.

Let me fill you in about our next-door neighbors Jane and John, now these two characters really took Mark and me for a loop. I notice that he was much older than Jane was and I did not give it much thought. Jane was kind enough to offer her babysitting services. At first, everything was great and then Samuel and Manuel started complaining and I thought they were just lying. One evening I arrived home from work and Jane said to me "don't worry, I fed the kids dinner already and they are fine". I thanked Jane for all her kindness and I asked the kids what they had for dinner.

Samuel said that Ms. Jane had ordered a pizza for the children for dinner and this bitch made my children watch her kids eat pizza and made Samuel and Manuel have bread with mayonnaise.

Why did this evil bitch do this? Jane was extremely lucky I did not put my foot in her ass. I never questioned why, I always thought that there was a reason evil people would follow me. Was I evil in my past life? For some reason I do not quite understand why people wanted to mistreat my babies and me.

Jane went on an attack mode through the entire neighborhood, I was called every name in the book and many people would not speak to me because of how small-minded they were. This horrible woman blacked-balled me and through the years, I stayed to myself.

The horrible gossip of this sad pathetic woman, one of my neighbors never truly got a chance to know me. Jane's mother, God rest her soul, never got a chance to know who I really was. Many people saw through Jane's ridiculous nonsense. I felt blessed to have met some wonderful neighbors of mine. During the time with the drama with Ms. Jane, things in my marriage were not so great and I kept my feelings deep inside. There was so much yelling and screaming; I prayed there had to be a better way to communicate with my husband. During our yelling, I would be slapped. You see, you could not go up against Mark; he had the last word and if I tried to disagree with him, I was slapped. I have been hit so many times that I just cannot remember all of the abuse. It would be too much for one person to handle emotionally.

Did I block it out of my memory? My boy's would remember things and I would say, "Why can't I remember that day?" Manuel would say, "Mom I remember."

I was now marked, I committed adultery and no matter how hard I tried, nothing I said would ever change these past indiscretions.

Star started dating Dick and not long after that, Star relocated to Indiana and they were married, just like most men like Mark and Dick, it's all about control, I never truly believed Dick loved Star. He wanted to control her like he had in most of his past relationships.

Sadly, we did not stay in touch as much as I wished. He did not want Star to communicate with me. Dick was evil and controlling as well, I just prayed that one day we would see each other again. Later on, I found out that Star was also a victim of domestic violence. When she tried to tell Mark what her husband was doing to her, Mark did not believe her. I knew why Mark did not believe her, he was an abuser himself and he would be admitting to the horrible abuse he put me through.

Mark and Dick were childhood friends; they were both controlling, abusive mentally & physically and outright assholes. Star was heartbroken.

The love that I saw in Star for Tim Best stayed in my memory and I deeply felt for her. The interference between Star's family and Tim's family made my head spin. There was constant interference from both families; couldn't they see what I saw, the love that they felt for one another? I blame them because ever since that time poor Star and Tim never found happiness; the happiness they deserved and lost so many years ago!

I continued to take on temporary positions and I started working for Reliance Insurance Company. During the time of my employment with them, I met Daisy. Daisy was a graduate from an Ivy League School and she treated me with the utmost respect, Daisy did not care that I was the receptionist.

Daisy and I became hanging buddies and at first, we would just stop by this little place under the Concourse and have drinks. I have to admit that I would forget the time. Truthfully, I just did not want to go home and I knew my babies were safe. When I think of it now, the love between Mark and I was supposed to have blossomed into something wonderful, but it did not. This is how I thought of Mark, the love of my life and because of the abuse from the very beginning of our marriage, I slipped into this deep dark hole.

When I did hang out too late, I paid for it later on. Mark's physical abuse never stopped and time after time, I would have to make up a lie about my bruises. I told lie after lie about my bruises. I would go into hiding. I would call my parents and act as though everything was just wonderful, which it was not.

Daisy and I started hanging out in nightclubs and I guess this is what you would call my selfish phase. Shit, I behaved as though I was a single woman. Mark would babysit for Daisies little girl, Karen. He would also stay at home with our children. I thought Daisy and I had a great friendship; I was so wrong.

Even after my affair, I wanted to see a marriage counselor and Mark refused. Mark said, "I am not going to allow anyone to tell me how to run my marriage". This is exactly the same way he told my parents. I realized there was nothing I could do. Time moved on, I continued to work for the company, and Mark trusted me less and less. We would argue more and more and he would hit me repeatedly. One of my memories of the abuse was when I told him of my affair. He gathered the kids into the bedroom and he asked them how much do you love your mother" They said, "We love mom a lot". His next question was, "How would you feel if your mother died and went away?" They said, "We would be very upset!" With that, Mark smacked me so hard across the face that my contact flew right out of my eye. My boy's remember witnessing Mark banging my head up against the bathroom wall. I just do not remember this abuse taking place because there were so many times it happened that I suppressed many of the incidences.

Many times Mark and I would argue repeatedly. If I did not agree with him, he would hit. Maybe deep down in his heart he did not care for me anymore, this is something that I will never know. One evening we were in the bedroom and we were arguing when he put his hands over my nose and mouth and I couldn't breathe. I really believe this was the day Mark was going to kill me at that moment. During my struggle with him, I believed that I was going to die and I wondered what would happen to my children; what about my boys? I was not so concerned about my daughter Elizabeth because she had her father. However, I worried about my boys.

My boy's remember how he grabbed my head and banged it up against the bathroom wall and how my son's would come barging into the room when they would hear their father and I struggling.

Because of the shame and guilt that I felt because of my affair, Mark thought he was entitled to what most men want. Yes, he wanted a threesome and he wanted the threesome with another woman. Maybe he knew that if I did this with her it would bring me pain because I was so close to this other woman.

We did not have a threesome, it was just me watching them have sex and I was sick and distraught. I felt like this dark hole was becoming my prison and there was no escaping; I felt doomed.

Even after that night each time my close friend would come to visit, Mark thought he was going to sleep with her and my insides were ripping me apart. I would say to Mark "what do you think that, every time she comes to visit your going to have sex with her? I believe in my heart we both felt horrible about all of this and we never spoke about it again but I don't think my close friend ever looked at me the same or respected me the same. Who would?

I did not feel the same way about myself. How useless I felt, how I felt I was not woman enough for my husband. My close friend had sex with my husband and I had to watch! Who would respect me after that?

My career with Insurance Company lasted until 1987 and as much as I tried to advance with the company, it just did not happen. I took courses in computer and insurance. In our building alone, there were only two Latino's and one worked in data processing. Victoria and I would chat at times in the language we grew up speaking, Spanish. One afternoon we were told that we were not allowed to speak our native language in the office. Victoria and I were both stunned and I knew it was time for me to leave.

I decided to give my two-week notice, Mark was very upset with me, and I told him I had to do this for my best

72

interest. Not long after I left Reliance, I applied for a position with Globe Security on Lombard Street. I interviewed with Lora Di Santro and from the very beginning, Lora and I became great and wonderful friends. I could not believe my luck. I also met William Vernon and we were like the three musketeers. We looked out for each other, they were more than just my co-workers they became my second family.

Working for Globe Security was one of my happiest times in my employment history and in my life. I felt appreciated and respected by these two wonderful people and how blessed I am to have met them. Going to work was like going to group therapy and my bosses were my supporters. During my employment with Globe, the abuse continued if I did not agree with Mark he continued to hit and I would say "the difference between you and I is that, I can admit when I am wrong, you can never admit when you're wrong"! Mark never felt he was wrong, he was the boss and we were his slaves. He would call the boys his slaves. Our home was his country, he was the dictator, and he had the last word.

During the time with the company, the investigation department wanted to hire me as a private investigator but Mark would not permit it or even when I was with the insurance company, I wanted to attend paralegal school and he was angry because he thought I was being selfish. Mark said, "What about me and the kids?" Therefore, my dreams of becoming a paralegal died and with that, I fell deeper into my dark hole.

After a year or so, the company went through reorganization and I was let go. After I left Globe Security, I took some time off to be with Mark and the kids. By that time Mark was promoted to Sergeant for the, Philadelphia Police Department and he was preparing for Lieutenant Exam. Mark's family always said that I was going to hold Mark back, he would never advance on the Police Department. I promised myself as his wife, partner, soul mate and friend Mark would move up in rank and I would give him all the support that he needed.

Mark's abuse at times would leave a blank space in my memory. My children would remember how, often I asked myself why, did I forget so many abusive memories.

During the fall of 1986, Mark and a couple of sergeants were all studying for the Lieutenant Exam. I was still with the Insurance Company and every morning my schedule was to be up by five so I could make it in time for work. I did not have my driver's license so I depended on public transportation. My travel consisted of a bus and the Broad Street Subway, so it took me more than an hour to get to work.

Mark got home quite early in the morning after one of his study groups while I was in a deep sleep. When I finally realized what was going on I awoke and realized that my husband was on his knees and he smelled of alcohol as he started kissing me and crying. I thought something horrible had happen to his grandmother. I said, "Mark what's wrong, did something happen". Mark started crying even more as he began to tell me the story about one of his study group friends who just happened to be a female. Mark said he felt so sorry for her and I asked him, "Why do you feel sorry for her?" My husband began to tell me the story about this poor, sad and lonely woman.

This officer was having an affair with my husband's sergeant and she was so distraught and upset because he was not going to leave his wife. During the entire story Mark kept kissing me and holding me and I thought to myself, "Did something else happen?" I did not want to stress it any further so I just dropped the subject and we both went to sleep.

Until this horrible, Christmas Party. Mark's friend from the 4th district had invited us to their Christmas party, now try to picture this, there had to be at least five women all piled up in this little kitchen and as usual all the men were standing in the living room. One of the wives began to tell me a story. "Hey Carmen", she said, "Did you hear what happened at one of the study groups?" and I said, "No, what happen?" Well, the truth came out that Daniel and another police officer along with this female officer had a threesome. I slowly turned to look over at Mark and I could see that he knew I now figured it out because the next thing I know, he grabbed me by the arm and took me directly out of the house. Once we were in the car, I said to Mark, "You had sex with her and that other idiot." I did not yell because I know he would have hit me, but I remember that night so clearly. I said, "You came home crying about how sorry you felt for her and it was not because you felt sorry; it was because your guilt was overwhelming for you."

Mark denied it repeatedly! One thing I know about police officers is that they will stick to their story no matter what. Try to get them to tell the truth, the truth is their truth.

Daniel's wife gave him a choice, it was either the study group or her and Daniel choice was his wife. I am sure many people would ask why I stayed in this marriage for so long. I've heard from friends and family how, lucky I was, a man with no children accepted me and my children and love them as his own and I started believing the bullshit. How I allowed so many people to influence my thoughts and my worthiness.

Mark's, famous words was "I treat you like a queen". What a joke, I did not feel like a queen; I allowed Mark and so many other people to make me feel I was not important enough. My feelings were numb and so were my boys. Mark at times would tell our son that they were not going to amount to anything and what makes this so sad is they wanted his approval especially Manuel. Mark never took the time to realize how much Manuel wanted his love and support. My sad husband would call his son's his little slaves. Did he ever realize the affect this had on them or did he really care.

In the year of 1987, Mark left. I was working for the law firm Wander and Herb. I received a phone call from my husband who called to inform me that he left. "Mark said that he had moved out and he was not coming back." Oh my God, what a time and place to do this, I just started crying, my boss asked me if I needed to leave and of course, I said yes. Traveling home alone was unbearable, I could not even think straight. Mark saw me get dropped off by a male friend from work one evening and he thought I was having an affair and no matter what I said it did not matter, I was having sex with another man. Now most women would have been happy that their abuser left. This was my time for me to get help; I knew there was something wrong with me. I loved him and I did not realize the mental, emotional, and physical damage that had overwhelmed my life.

So many times while my abuser was hitting me, I felt that I deserved it but I wanted him back in my life. Why would I want him back when in my heart I kept telling myself that he did not love me?

My son's were so upset and poor little Manuel kept calling for him out the window. Even when they wanted to spend time with him he would question Samuel why didn't he look for his real father and poor Samuel would say," you are my real father". Mark never knew that our son repeated those words to me. The only father that they knew was gone and they wanted him back. One afternoon I had dropped the boys off to visit with their father and Margo made it a point to tell Samuel that as long as she is alive my children would never be thought of as her great grandchildren. Margo made it quite clear to my sons that they were not her blood. Mark told Samuel, "Don't tell your mother what Grandma Margo said". My husband did not protect our son's; he allowed the verbal and emotional abuse to continue to happen. Did my husband's family ever realize the pain that they caused, or did they care?

One evening I was so depressed and I started drinking heavily. The children called Mark and what did my husband do? He gave the police department the impression that I had my children held hostage. Before I knew it, the swat team was on top of the roof and posted outside with rifles pointed at my home.

Samuel kept crying saying that I did not have them hostage, I was just intoxicated. They didn't listen to him and took Mark's word because of the position he held in the police department.

Later on I was told that the swat team was not there to help me, their plan was to shoot and ask questions later. Elizabeth reminded me later that I was suicidal and I cannot help but to agree with her. The shame and guilt had over taken me and I felt there was no other way out other then death.

Mark tried to have me 302'd, which in police terms, are to have me committed to the mental hospital. No, they could not commit me, but Mark made it clear that if I ever expected for things work out for us I would have to voluntarily commit myself. So, foolish and naïve, I did exactly what Mark wanted.

I was admitted into Jefferson Hospital. I was there for five days and all I wanted to do was to be with my children. The doctor found nothing wrong with me and I knew there was nothing wrong with me. I was suffering from all the mental, physical and emotional abuse over so many years. Mark labeled me as crazy and this is how I was treated after that horrible night.

It was great to be home with the kids. Mark's brutality towards the boys and me was horrible. His famous words were that we were stupid and we were never going to amount to nothing. I tried to correct the damage and I tried to tell these wonderful son's of mine that he was wrong. "Please don't listen to him", I said; and the heart wrenching guilt of not being able to help my babies as I should have. It was an overwhelming sadness. The pain was inconceivable. I was their mother, I am supposed to have protected my children and I allowed this man to treat them like nothing. How could I allow this to happen? What type of man would do this to two little boys who wanted his love and approval? What type of person did that make me?

I made a promise to myself that I would not allow this to happen again. I started counseling with Dr. Gilles and as a family, we all started attending sessions. Samuel and Elizabeth would talk and we would look to Manuel to talk but he just refused. I just did not realize how much this affected my son Manuel.

Mark was Manuel's hero. My little boy would draw comic book pictures of his father in his SWAT uniform or in a regular police uniform. Manuel wanted to be a police officer just like his dad. Sadly, Mark made it quite clear to Manuel that he would not recommend him for the police department and he broke Manuel's heart.

After that, Manuel's feelings towards his father changed. Manuel was once the little guy who thought the world of his father, later he became a troubled man.

Mark and I allowed Manuel's elementary school to convince us to have him committed to the Friend's Hospital, it was a Children's Psychiatric Hospital. Mark, being the "man" of the house had the last say and decided that Manuel would be admitted.

The doctors at Friend's Hospital found nothing wrong with my son. He was just a hyperactive young man with a lot of energy. What is quite clear to me now is that my son was more than likely, riddled with anxiety. The damage and long-lasting effects on our children's emotional well-being is something we will never know. Mark or I surely never realized it at the time; but, being that I am their mother, it will always weigh on my mind. The doctors described my Manuel as an above average child. My baby could have gone so far and the damage from the abuse hurt him so much.

Later, one afternoon while Mark and I were separated, Doris was on the phone with the boys and they wanted to talk to their father. They wanted to see him. Well, the next thing Doris told the boy's was that I had slept with six different men! They were crushed to hear what their grandmother had said to them, both of them were crying uncontrollably.
How could this women be so cruel, where is her soul? A schoolteacher, what type of person would be so vile to children, to my children. My god not only did I protect Mark from the abuse we sustained. The emotional abuse that Doris instilled into my children is unforgivable and one day I pray she will have to ask God to forgive her, not me. I feel no hate, just pity for her. Yes, I admit it, I had affairs each time Mark would hit me and I would run into another man's arms. I realize I did not like myself and I did not like the men I had affairs

with. Was I trying to fill a void in my soul? What was I searching for?

Mark was supposed to be their father, my husband and our friend. He was not around and I thought that maybe one day he would realize what horrible memories these boys have.

Mark had so much to learn when it came to our sons. Elizabeth was such a different issue. Elizabeth became very ill and was admitted into the hospital and Mark stayed with her during the entire time she was there. Our sons always felt their father treated Elizabeth better. All they wanted from Mark was his approval and respect.

One afternoon Mark came by the house. As usual, we were arguing about him returning home and things just became uglier. Mark and I were sitting in his car and I looked down and saw a phone number with the name Kristen on it. When I went to lift up the piece of paper, that is when Mark grabbed me and we were struggling and the next thing I know, I was punched on the side of my face. Mark was wearing his high school ring and with that, my right side of my face had a large lump and I was black and blue for weeks. My boys arrived home and they saw my face and began to cry. My goodness, did we ever realize what kind of lasting affect this would have on our family. I will take responsibility for the horrible things that went wrong in my marriage, but often I would wonder if Mark would ever do the same. I cheated, time and time again. I hated the abuse and I hated myself. I thought the only way I could find the love I was looking for was to sleep with another man. Well, that's bullshit!

During the time of our separation, I did everything I could think of to keep me busy and began fixing the house. I painted, removed the rugs, and stripped the floors. I spent a lot of time with the kids. We would go to the Park. I tried my best to make things happy for all of us. We all wanted Mark back home and Mark knew this but when I think about it now it was a major mistake. Our suffering through all of this was just too much for any human spirit. I remember one afternoon, I told Mark that he had to take the boys for a bit and he refused. I will take responsibility for this but will Mark ever? Mark and I were going to hand them over to child welfare and I was so distraught that I could not think straight. I walked out of the building and sat across the street for about five minutes. Then I went right back in and took my children home. Until this day, I have been trying to erase the pain that my poor little boys suffered. Their education suffered greatly and all I wanted the best for my sons.

Mark returned 8 months later and we all thought it was the best news in the world. Now his mother and grandmother were so angry. The Thanksgiving when he returned the children and I attended Thanksgiving Dinner at Mark's cousin Troy's home. Troy obviously had a bit too much to drink and proceeded to tell me exactly how they all felt. They did not want us together, period. During the time, Mark and I reconciled our marriage, I was working for Bally's Fitness Center and he was now Lt. for the Swat Team. I was working twelve-hour days and it was putting a strain on our marriage again. Therefore, because my position was not as important as Mark's we both decided that it would be a good idea that I resign my position and take care of our children and our home. Mark was now preparing to start a new study group for the position of Captain.

I wanted to do everything to please my husband, I cooked, cleaned, washed, painting, god help me who was I kidding I did it all, even when we went to the shore, Mark wanted a surfboard; I bought him a surfboard. Anything to make him happy, god help me, I was not happy and I went further into my dark, black hole. I recall one his buddies came into our home while I was busy sanding down the floors and his comment to Mark was "you have her trained", back then all I could do was laugh it off but deep down it caused me so much sadness.

Mark never had to worry about anything at home, I was there, I made sure the kids went off to school, dinner was always fixed, the house was kept clean I even tried my best to do the carpentry work around the house, though I was not a carpenter. I did everything a wife was supposed to do, or so I thought. It was just not ever enough.

I knew that Mark wanted his family to respect his decision to make our marriage work. After Thanksgiving dinner with the family and him never making a comment on the remarks that were made, I realized things were going to continue to be the same. No matter what I tried to do for us as a family, it would never make a difference to Mark's family.

The anxiety and fear of Mark leaving again overwhelmed me and I never felt secure in my marriage ever again. Deep down I knew he was going to leave again and I was afraid of the affect it would have on my little family. There were times I felt that I was being foolish and that I worried too much, but it was my reality.

Our Christmas dinners were spent at our home and we would take separate days to invite our families. My nephew Daniel would tease me he would say, "Titi Lola, I remember when you did not even like to cook".

Mark had an identity crisis during our marriage. One minute he wanted to be a Harley Davidson biker and even dressed like one, but he did not have a bike. Then he wanted to be a cowboy with the whole ensemble of boots, hats, and shirts (ha, ha, ha, ha). Oh, but he did not have a horse. Then he wanted to be a surfer. I bought him a surfboard but Mark was a big guy so he bought himself a 10ft Chuck Dent surfboard. I believe his last identity crisis is when he started taking dancing lessons and people would call him the "Mambo King." Not that he was an outstanding dancer, but it was a name many of his friends would call him behind his back.

I loved dancing. I was taught as a child to dance salsa, meringue, and many other dances. I did a complete turnaround in my marriage. I thought if I concentrated on my home and my family things would be so much happier.

Daniel, my nephew, was so right about me not wanting to cook. It was so much work on top of everything else I was trying to do. Daniel had lived with us for a bit while he was attending school to be an electrician. He was my "bodyguard" and we would take the bus together to class and then take it back home.

One afternoon, my nephew and I did not have class and Mark was home. They were both watching television when Mark heard water splashing in the basement, Mark went running downstairs and the hose from the washing machine had snapped off. There was water all over the floor and Mark reached for the light switch on the ceiling while he was standing in water. Well, guess what happened next? Yes, he got the electrical shock of his life.
Mark was very lucky. My nephew could not believe what he did and he said, "Mark's hair was standing up and that just made me laugh." God, I am so sorry that it just made me laugh too!

Now, not much longer after that horrible accident, it happened again. I thought he would be much smarter this time around. Well, I was wrong. I always use to say that for such a smart man, he truly surprised the heck out of me. This time the electrical shock knocked his ass into the door.

During this brief time in our lives, Delia had relocated to Texas and wore out her welcome, and then she ended up in Florida, with her new man Dick. She came out for Mark's promotion to Sergeant and at that time, my sister-in-law was expecting her second child. It was at this time that Delia met Mica, our neighbor. She also gave birth to her second child, Ken.

Let me step back a bit, before Delia left for California my mother-in-law convinced Delia to give up her first born son, Little Jordon, to his father. My mother-in-law was giving the impression that she would be allowed by "Big Jordon" to see her grandson. Well, Doris was so wrong. Jordon and his family made it clear that Doris would never see her grandson again.

When Delia decided to relocate to Texas, I'm sure she never dreamed she would not be able to see her son. In a million years, this would never happen. I often wondered how little Jordon was going through all those years but...I was only married into the family so with that I would have to keep my thoughts to myself.

Delia was living the life style of the rich and famous, the new love of her life gave her a Porsche to drive, did not have to worry about going hungry and had everything her little heart desired.

During the time Delia was living with Carlo she was traveling back and forth with a nanny and with Mica. Both Mica and Delia were traveling back and forth to the islands. Delia paid his bills and bought a van that he needed for his side work. Come to think of it, Delia was his sugar mommy and he was enjoying every bit of it.

Please do not get me wrong, I felt no jealousy towards my sister-in-law.

Every single time Delia was into some sort of scam, or her love life was a mess, there was always some way that we were dragged into it. I could not tell my husband to keep her nonsense out of our lives because he would become very angry. I could never be jealous of Mark and his family because I spent too many years caught up in all of their drama.

Mark never realized how much I wanted the love and respect of his family. He would say, "It's you and I and they have nothing to do with our marriage." They constantly interfered in our lives, time and time again.

Mark once asked Delia for some help during a time when I was between jobs. Delia was always about just Delia and the men that came in and out of her life. Helping out her brother was the farthest thing from her mind. I could see the pain and sadness in my husband's face.

One weekend Delia and Mica had just returned from one of the islands and Mica had invited us over to his place. Delia had invited another couple that were very good friends of hers. Mark and I did not know them and had just met them for the first time. If my life depended on it, I could not remember the woman's name. However, I will always remember his name. It was Juan.

Juan and his girlfriend seemed to be having a couple's issue and we became their audience. Alcohol seems to bring out the worst in people so Mark became tired of it all, it was nonsense. He became angry at his sister and decided to leave. Mica lived across the street from us, so when I got tired of it all, I could leave.
Juan and his girlfriend went inside Mica's house and I remember we were standing in the kitchen and the argument continued. I was walking back outside and I

looked up to see Juan standing on the steps still arguing with his girlfriend and in Spanish I told Juan to please stop that. He was in this man's home and I knew in my heart that Mica was about to do something.

Just as I was calming Juan down, along came Mica and the next words that came out of his mouth stunned both Juan and I. Mica said, "I don't want that Spanish speaking shit in my house!" Juan and I turned and just looked and I said to Mica "Mica, I was trying to calm him down. Do you realize what you just said?" Mica told me to get the fuck out of his house and as I was walking down the stairs he started arguing with me and of course, I returned words back at him. The next thing I knew he wanted to hit me. I looked at him and said "If you value your job and badge you will think twice about what you are about to do."

I walked back across the street to my home and I told Mark what had happened. As usual, Mark said and did nothing. Not long after this horrible incident, the police were all over Mica's house. Sadly, Mica took his shotgun and hit Juan over the head. Juan had to be taken to the hospital with a huge gash on his head. Instead of asking me what had taken place earlier, the police arrested Juan. Mica tried to apologize to me but from there on our relationship as neighbors was not so great.

This just showed me time and time again how abusive police officers can be and how they use their position to abuse. I thought it was normal, but how wrong I was. How could society continue to ignore how many police officers are very abusive and how many people like me continued to suffer.

Carlo and Delia's relationship became strained so one weekend Mark and Mica flew from Philadelphia to Texas to pick up her Porsche. The car didn't even belong to Delia. In fact, the car belonged to Carlo. Well, Mark and

Mica drove back from Texas to Philadelphia. Carlo became aware of all the spending Delia was doing and how this woman was able to convince her brother and Mica to pick up the car. Carlo was just about to give her the boot when the great news came out that Delia was expecting another child.

Delia returned home with Carlo and things looked like they were working out. Deep down I always felt that Delia was looking for someone or something. I could just never quite put my finger on it. She was the type of woman who believed that if you looked a certain way you should be able to live the life of the rich and famous.

I cannot remember exactly when it happened; I know I was working for Globe Security. Mark accused me of cheating but I was not. Mark he hit me again. I was talking on the phone later to Delia and it was her who sent me a plane ticket to go fly out to Chicago and visit with my brother Ralph. When I told my mother-in-law about the abuse she asked, "What did you do to Mark to make him hit you?" It seems her memory had failed her because I remember the words coming out of her own mouth that my father-in-law had once broken her arm. "What had she done?" I thought to myself.

Many people caused me so much pain and I remember with amazement. I would hear these horrible words come out of their mouths and no matter how much healing there is the memories of abuse will always be there. Just a story will cause me to flash back by triggering a memory from my past.

Not long after Victor was born and poor Carlo's business went under, money got very tight for him and Delia again. Their relationship was now ending. Much to our surprise Fred Rodriquez, a baseball player for the St. Louis Cardinals, became Delia's new boyfriend.

There was a call from Delia and she wanted us to meet Fred. She also wanted me to cook a dinner for us all and for me to fix some beans and my Spanish chicken stew for Fred. I was always proud of my cooking, and so I did.

We met Delia and Fred at a downtown hotel where all the professional baseball and football players go. We were sitting in the lobby of the bar having drinks. Fred and I started talking in Spanish, Delia earlier asked me to feel him out and I did. So, we are sitting here and I can tell he was your typical old fashion Latino man. He expects his wife or girlfriend to do everything from cooking, cleaning, and keeping your mouth shut. Come to think of it, men who are controlling and abusive think this way. This is why Mark did not like Fred because Fred reminded Mark of himself.

When Delia and I finally were alone and she wanted my opinion about Fred, I sat her down and I proceeded to tell her about Fred. I said "Delia don't mess with this one. He is an old fashion Latino man and he does not play." I tried to advise her the best way I knew how and with my last words. I did not address it ever again.

It wasn't long after we met Fred and attended one of his games against the Philadelphia Phillies that he and Delia were married.

I was happy for Delia because I hoped that maybe this was the one. Delia was back in Philly for a bit while Fred was playing ball. I was kind enough to watch over little Victor while Delia and Fred were on their honeymoon. Victor was such a cutie and I love being with him. I remember I would fix him cream of wheat and he loved it. I was always concerned about the little guy because he was kind of small. He was so little and my mother and I were always trying to fatten him up.

Fred had relocated Delia and the boys to Indiana and things seemed good until I received that phone call from

Fred. One of Delia's friends, Marsha, was visiting and Fred proceeded to tell me what was going on. Fred, said "Carmen, I bought everything for the house, pots and pans, everything to cook with, and all Delia wants to do is go out and spend money, I am sending her back".

So with that, Fred gave Delia $2,000.00 dollars and shipped her right back to Philadelphia, PA and because they were not married very long, Delia was not entitled to single dime.

I did not know what to say to Fred, I felt for Delia. Delia came home to Philadelphia, PA and once again, she moved in with us. We did not have much room and we tried to make it the best way we could. Delia relocated to Kansas for a bit. The boy's were able to see their father and Delia was working, but she got into some trouble out there and Mark had to speak to the police department in Kansas.

Now during her time in Kansas, Delia met Samuel Bones. Samuel was much older than her and married. Not long after that, Gem came along and Delia was in a financial strain. Now of course you must be wondering what was going on with Mark and I through all of this. Mark was concentrating on his career and his sister's nonsense, so, I had to deal with the soap opera of my in-law and keep my mouth shut. Do you think I kept my thoughts and my silence to myself, no I didn't.

There was so much arguing with my husband that it just put a bigger and bigger strain on our marriage. I remember Mark taking time off from work to fly his nephew home. Or when we would travel to pick up mom's mail from her PO Box, when the smart thing to do was leave it there! I never completely understood any of it.

Mark never realized or he just did not care about the nonsense his family had brought into our home and when we argued, I would get smacked. How pathetic my marriage had become and how small of a person I had become.

Mark confused me so much. One minute I was selfish then he would say what's wrong with you? You don't do anything anymore. I just did not understand why he was doing this to me. I thought he would be happy if I just did not go anywhere. He was controlling my life and I felt like I was going completely mad. I came to realize I was never going to be good enough of a women, lover or friend. I was just a piece of flesh that was trying to exist.

Our son Samuel was diagnosed with cataracts when he was 14 years old. The doctor's did not understand why, myself, Elizabeth and Samuel all inherited the Cataract disease. Samuel was the first patient at his young age to receive implants in the eyes. Never did I questioned our God about why, only to say, please bless us with some sight.

For the next six years, I was tending to our home and watching the kids while Mark worked two jobs. He worked for the police department and he worked at times for a law firm as a bodyguard. Mark was trying to make ends meet and at that time, I thought he really cared for the kids and me. I wanted so much to please him; I did not want him to worry about the kids. So, I tried my best for all of us.

Grandmother Margo was getting up in age and my mother-in-law felt that it would be best that they sold the house on 46th Street. Mark was so upset that his childhood memories were in this wonderful house. Mark felt that as long as the home was a part of the family his grandfather's memory would live on forever.

On March 21, 1994, I was not quite myself and I had such a sad feeling that had come over me. Then I received the phone call. My father's voice came over the receiver and I can tell that something was wrong. I asked my Papi what's was wrong and he said "Junior" and I said "what about Junior?" I could not believe what my father said next "Junior died". All I could hear were my screams and dropping down to the floor. This was not happening, not again, I could not believe the horrible pain that took over me. Mark looked over at me and I told him what happened, he could not believe it either. I know Mark loved Junior and Junior loved him.

Junior never knew Mark was abusing me from the first year of our marriage. I was so ashamed because I couldn't tell my family. They thought Mark was the best thing since Coca Cola.

Mark and I rushed to Camden where my sister lived and we rushed right to Cooper Medical Hospital. In the waiting room were my mother, father, and my sister Edwina. They all looked shocked and out of the compassion from the staff I was allow into the room. Lying there was a part of my life and I could not believe this was happening again! My brother Arturo died fourteen years earlier, now Junior.

In this horrible time of my life, Mark was a great support and I cannot thank him enough. God, how I wish things could of always been like this. How we supported, comforted, and were there for one another. There will always be memories of happy times and horrible times.

My entire family was devastated and overwhelmed with grief. We could not believe we lost Junior. I often wonder where I got this strength to sit down and discuss funeral arrangements while the rest of the family argued. I felt that my entire being was all in slow motion. I picked out the last garment that I would see my nephew wear and what he would be buried in. My sister Edwina needed help and I would scrub walls before the family came to visit after the funeral.

The entire time during the funeral and helping my sister with her house, I felt another piece of me died. My heart kept telling me my only purpose for being here was to make sure that my children were raised and they know how much I loved them.

Many people paid their last respects to Junior. All I could do was cry and question over and over again, "why?" Why was this happening to us again? When Arturo died, I was never the same. Arturo would say to me "Lola take care of your kids, they're all you have". Another famous saying of Arturo was "Never sink down to their level, you're better then that". I will always cherish the memory and the love of my brother Arturo ad now my nephew, Junior.
My sister, Marcia is a strong and hotheaded woman. I can laugh about this now, but wow! Daisy was kind enough to prepare Lasagna and there were plenty of people but not plenty of food. I guess during a death I could sit back and look because we all were emotional. We are not even aware of how hotheaded some families may get until a tragedy happens.

Grandma Margo moved into her own apartment and it was quite nice. Margo seemed very happy but she was also becoming ill. One afternoon while I was home cleaning I received a phone call from the management from the apartment complex. They were trying to locate my mother-in-law and Mark and to no avail; they had no luck in finding them. The management asked me if I was related to Margo and I said "YES!" She is my husband's grandmother.

I rushed over to the apartment complex and they let me in. Margo had an accident all over the rug and on her nightgown and in her bedroom. Grandma was able to clean herself but she needed help in cleaning up the waste in the apartment. I first washed her nightgown then I got on my hands and knees and started scrubbing the rugs in the living room and in the bedroom. After I made sure that everything was clean, I stayed with her for a bit. Margo said she was fine so I drove back home.

I often wonder through the years how cruel this woman was to my sons and me but something in my heart would not allow me to be cruel to her. Margo needed my help and no matter what happened during my marriage, I helped her.

Before Grandma Margo had her accident Doris had a birthday party for her and many of her old friends and family were there. The children and I were all sitting there and Grandma Margo proceeded to introduce us. Grandma Margo made it quite clear that I was his wife but these were not his kids. The children were getting older now and all we could do was walk out of the house and Mark said nothing. He did not come to our defense and he did not protect his family. As always, he let his grandmother say things to hurt the children and me. I prayed for many, many years that they would soften their hearts, but they never did.

When I would think of my mother-in-law, I thought of her as a lie to the world. She would attend church every week, sing on the choir, portrayed herself as a soft spoken, sweet, wonderful lady. But to my sons she was cruel and she did not show them love. She was called Grandma, but the love of a grandmother was never there.

I can finally say the physical abuse continued but the emotional and mental abuse was driving me mad. I wanted out of life. I wanted to just leave this world because I could not endure the pain anymore. Time continued on.

Grandma Margo's health had worsened and sadly, she had a stroke. Delia was back in town and my mother-in-law and Aunt Ana had rented a house for her in Chestnut Hill. Delia would visit grandma on a regular basis and I thought how sweet of her, but there was more to her visit than meets the eye. Delia had ordered new credit cards in Margo's name without her knowledge and put her name on them. Now you wonder how Delia was able to do this without my mother-in-law being aware of the theft. Delia would often visit and intercept the mailman and catch the bills coming in. Grandma Margo's long time lover Mr. Tubb's had passed away and left her some money. No one wanted Delia to know that Grandma Margo received this money from her long time lover.

I'm sure you may be wondering why my sister-in-law became such a big part of this story. It is because somehow, some way, her nonsense always ended up on our doorstep; either through her doing or through my mother-in-law's doing, their drama always played a part in our lives.

I am amazed at all the times and troubles we had. Reminds me of when it was time to relocate grandma to a nursing home. All the credit charges that Delia had charged were coming from every direction. Delia's expensive taste cost Mark's grandma Margo more than $60,000.00. Doris and Uncle Ed had no choice but to pay it because they did not want Delia to be arrested, or should I say, Doris did not want Delia arrested.

So, Delia's behavior was affecting the family again but the excuses they made simply blew my mind. Every single time Delia would do something illegal, they continued to find justification. I just watched and listened.

Mark and I continued to visit Grandma Margo frequently at the nursing home. Her behavior towards African American people was out of control.

Grandma Margo's bitterness towards dark skinned people continued in her old age. I was always apologizing to the staff because Margo kept calling them "Nigger". I was so embarrassed and the staff was so kind. This hateful lady would not stop. I did not want her to get hurt; I just could not get her to stop.

Delia had a new man in her life and his name was Greg. Greg was a young man and they had just recently met. Greg was so sure Delia came from money. One afternoon Delia arranged a huge birthday party for Greg at Book Binders. I watched my husbands' facial expression completely change as the wine and champagne was being served while Delia handed Greg his birthday gift. Mark realized that the money that was left to his grandmother Margo was being spent on his sister's new boyfriend.

Mark was pissed off and he began to drink heavily. Greg the delusional idiot, proposed. Delia gladly accepted. Yeah! Greg thought that Delia had made a settlement with her daughter's father and that she was given a nice amount. So, with that, the wedding was planned. Greg's mother just thought that Delia was wealthy and I kept telling them that Delia is not wealthy. This crazy bitch did it! She told Greg's mother not to listen to me because I was crazy. Delia went so far as to tell them that Mark had committed me into a mental hospital. I could not believe what this rotten bitch said to them. There wasn't much I could say or do. If I confronted Delia about this Mark would say I was confrontational. So, the hurt and pain just sank me further into my black hole. If the abuse was not physical, it was emotional. I could not understand any of this. Why did Mark continue to say I was negative?

I decided to stay to myself and watch what was going to happen next. The wedding went on, Delia and the wedding party stayed at the Four Seasons. Oh! It was a fancy wedding for the rich and the famous. Yes, I am being sarcastic when I say this.

Greg and Delia relocated to Voorhees, New Jersey. Greg was driving a black Mercedes, Delia had a huge Lexus SUV. The home had everything in it. Delia was working for two NFL Players. They took trips to Aruba. Everyone I know would like to live the dream of this life style, but Mark and I knew something was not right. Her son Jordon was back in her life.

Delia continued to shower Jordon with so many gifts and life was great, for now!

Mark knew Delia was involved in something dirty and he told his mother, but they always made justifications for whatever Delia did. This was the type of behavior that was acceptable within this family. They were above all people no matter what color skin you were. You know come to think of it, he would not admit to this but every time his sister Delia did something, Doris would call him and he was affected. I was affected and my children were affected. Over and over again, Delia's nonsense affected our family and Mark did not realize that it continued to enter our home.

The drama was in our home and the bullshit came right along with it. Greg was not working and things started getting strained. Delia had left to go visit her cousin in DC and when she returned from her little trip Greg had left and took a lot of their belongings with him. I did not feel sorry for her. Then the news finally hit the fan. It turned out that all this money that Delia apparently had with her new position with the two NFL Players was false. Delia had embezzled hundreds of thousands of dollars from these two players and she was busted. The FBI became involved and Delia was charged with embezzlement. Jordon testified against her and my mother-in-law was beside herself. My mother-in-law yelled at her grandson for telling the truth. This is going to sound familiar as I continue forward.

Delia was out on bail during the time of her hearing, and was looking for her next victim. Delia's next target was Mark's buddy Butch, but Butch would not date Mark's sister because he had too much respect for his friend. Next, she met Tom, who seemed like a very nice person. In April of 1994, we received a phone call from Delia that grandma's health had become worse and it was a matter of time. Mark and I went to the nursing home and both Delia and Tom were there. Delia did not want to stay, she was expecting her fifth child. Mark and I along with Doris, stayed with Grandma Margo. Mark and Doris fell asleep while I stayed at her bedside. I would touch her hand and I did not want her to feel she was alone. All through the night, I sat there just touching her hand and at 5:15 am, I could tell Margo was leaving us. I woke Mark and his mother to tell them Margo was leaving, but they did not believe me until the nurse came in and told them exactly what I had tried to tell them.

Margo S. Andrews, died at 5:30 that morning. I cried because I always wanted her approval and her love for the children and me. At the end of her life, Margo did show me some compassion and respect but I never truly felt the love that I hoped and prayed for.

Uncle Ed did not make it in time to say good-bye to his mother. He thanked me for staying with her and never leaving her side. I was extremely grateful to Uncle Ed thanking me for being there for his mother. I thought maybe, just maybe, they finally accepted me and respected me.

My children did not mourn her death and out of love and respect for Mark, they attended Margo's funeral services. During the services, the priests mentioned the family and those who were left behind. My children names were not a part of those left behind and I was mentioned by a man's name. I always knew that God was trying to tell me something. Why didn't I listen to him?

My sister Marcia came to the service to support me because I had an uneasy feeling. Marcia finally realized that there was something wrong with Mark's family and the way they treated the kids and me. My Manuel always had a healthy appetite and he kept going back for food and with that my mother-in-law made a horrible comment about how Manuel ate too much. Poor Manuel he had such an embarrassing look on his face. Both Marcia and I looked at one another and I knew no matter what I did for this woman it would never be enough. I would never receive the respect which I so deserved. My children would never receive the love that they deserved.

You wonder where Mark was, he was right there, the entire time he watched and listened to what his mother said. I am blessed to have my sister. It is because of her that I made it through the entire funeral service.

Before Delia met Tom, Delia had to do some time in prison. I took care of her daughter Alice as a favor to Mark and his mother. Alice would sleep in our daughter Elizabeth's room and we made sure Alice had a positive and Merry Christmas. I did this for Alice and for Mark because no child should have to go through a horrible Christmas while there mother is in prison. I did not want their approval and I knew by now that I would never receive the respect and acceptance from my mother-in-law.

Losing my nephew and my brother Arturo to drugs was so difficult. A deep hole had taken over my spirit and it was swallowing me up more and more. I remained in that dark hole for years after the death of my love ones.

After the passing of Margo and my nephew Junior, I promised Junior that I would attend Dan's football games. Mark and I would go to see him play in the rain and snow when it was freezing cold. This was a time in our life that things seemed good. I knew that our sex life was never the same. God, how I remember at times when Mark would touch me that all I could do was cry and hide in the bathroom afterwards. Mark would always ask me what was I doing, I would just say that I needed to go to the bathroom. The emptiness and sadness had overwhelmed me and I just never could tell him what I was feeling. Mark would be very critical of me. Many times, he would say that I was too sensitive or too nice. Maybe I was, or maybe I wasn't; I just wanted the love and respect I deserved. I finally realized that I wanted love and respect from this family but I did not love myself.

I was so proud of Dan. I reached out to a Spanish newspaper here in Philadelphia, PA by the name of Al Dia. A wonderful story was written about Dan and not long after that, the President of City Council Milton Moran had given Dan a commendation and recognition for the fine work he was doing as a student of Woodrow Wilson High School. Several of us from my family attended the ceremony. My mother was so proud of Dan.

The editor from Al' Dia' once asked me if I would like to work for the Spanish Newspaper but I was more consumed with my home life and trying to make sure that Dan's recruitment went well. For months, I talked to so many head couches and recruiters. Mark tried to get tape from Dan's coach from high school and he was not cooperating. My God, when I think about it now, it was horrible. Both Mark and I reached out to the school district and finally he gave some high lights of his games and my husband edited so he could send off the tapes. Indiana University from Bloomington, Indiana, viewed the tapes and they really wanted Dan to attend Indiana University.

Many schools wanted Dan: Temple, University of Penn, UCLA, Maryland, and University of Pitt just to name a few and no matter how hard I tried to get more tapes on Dan; this head coach would not help me. Dan finally went to Indiana and I said to my nephew "do not commit to them." Just wait to see if we can visit the other schools. I must have called every school to try to get Dan a visit out there and sadly nothing. Dan committed to Indiana and I was happy but angry at the same time. I knew how much Dan wanted to see the other schools and because I did not receive the help from this horrible head coach of his, Dan gave his word as a gentleman.

It breaks my heart to say this but things did not work out for Dan in Indiana, he was not used to the area and he wanted to come back home. I would say, "Dan give it some time. Dan give it a chance." Unfortunately, Dan wanted to come home and he did. He played for Rowan University and his football career did not last.
Later I heard how the family blamed me for Dan's career ending and I blew them right off. I know that no matter what the family said, I did everything I could to help Dan and so did Mark. My love and support was there for him and the head coach from Indiana sent me a letter of gratitude for supporting my nephew through the change to Indiana.

I became Account Executive for Al' Dia' Newspaper and I very much enjoyed working for Herman. He was a very humble and modest person whom I respected very much. I also respected his newspaper.

One afternoon, I was on my way to see a client when my car broke down and I was stranded in New Jersey. Sadly, Mark could not pick me up because his vehicle was a Police vehicle and he could not take the car out of the State. I understood. Herman was kind enough to pick me up and get me back to Philly.

That weekend Mark and I went shopping for a car. Mark would always say I bought this car because of you. I did not want this car. However, I was working in New Jersey and I needed a reliable vehicle. Perhaps my husband did not feel I deserved a car. Who knows? Mark continued to move up in rank on the Police Department and I was quite happy with the newspaper.

My girlfriend Lora was preparing for her wedding. I was asked by Lora and her fiancé Bruce to translate the wedding from Spanish to English. The wedding ceremony was taking place in Cabo, Mexico and I was so excited and happy for Lora and Bruce. They were both wonderful people and Lora was always a true and wonderful friend to me and I felt so blessed to have her in my life.

I was excited about flying out to Mexico and as I was traveling back home to prepare to pack. I noticed from a distance that a huge black SUV was coming my way. Now as I remember they had the stop signs and I was so sure that they would stop! No one stopped and I was hit on the driver side of the vehicle and dragged about 800 feet. The air bag busted open and I could barely breathe but with the grace of GOD, somehow I was able to open my car door. At the time, I felt like a cat. How many more lives do I have left? Mark did rush to the accident scene and I felt extremely lucky because it could have been worse. My only concern was myself, and of course, my car. They were several young people who were out joy riding, the driver of the other vehicle was a young nineteen-year-old female. I yelled at her and the young woman continued to apologize. I stopped yelling. I was taken to the hospital and all in one piece.

I flew out to Cabo St. Lucas, Mexico a little bruised but ALIVE. My stay there was just wonderful and the entire time I wished Mark was there with me. Mark said we could not afford for him to fly out with me. I told Mark that Bruce and Lora would cover our hotel expenses, but he said we could not afford for him to come with me. I know now that this was a time when our marriage was failing and no matter what we both tried to do, it would never work.

The wedding ceremony was held on the edge of the ocean as I watched my beautiful girlfriend and her handsome husband stand in front of me. I could not translate the wedding vows; all I could do was cry. I cried out of happiness for them because they found one another and they both deserved the upmost happiness.

I was blessed to have such wonderful and positive people in my life such as Bruce and Lora Caton.

We drank that night away like fishes (ha, ha, ha, ha) and the next morning I had to fly back to the states. On the flight I had such a hangover that I could not keep my head up. My flight back to the states was a nightmare. We were caught in a horrible thunderstorm and I was so sure we were going to crash. I was sitting next to a Navy man and I felt like I was going to break his hand as hard as I squeezed it. When we finally landed in Philadelphia, PA, I thanked him for his compassion. I must have looked like hell because when Mark saw me all he could do was laugh at the way I looked. Initially, I was angry but when I think about it now, I can laugh it off.

I was back at work again at the newspaper and the confidence and respect that I felt was so wonderful.

When Mark was promoted to Captain his name was mentioned as the husband of one Al' Dia's employees and I was so proud. My name was printed as Carmen De La Rosa Stun and this was the day that I decided to take my maiden name as my middle name. I was so proud of myself. Not that I felt I was special, but the respect I received was wonderful and it felt great. I realized that I had a gift of being a great listener and I showed everyone I met the respect and appreciation they deserved. Herman asked me to meet with a gentleman who owned two Pharmacies in Camden. It was nice working in the old neighborhood. Memories of my school days and positive memories of my brother Arturo were great.

Mr. Pike was a man that was quite full of himself but I sat and gave him my undivided attention. Mr. Pike asked me to sit down. My plan was to talk about advertisements and to discuss what we could do to help him improve his advertising for the Pharmacies. Mr. Pike wanted me to see his plaques and trophies he received from schools and many more organizations. I thought to myself, how generous of him, not many companies are kind enough to give so much to the school children of Camden, New Jersey.

I realize that our meeting had gone on longer then I planned and I politely interrupted Mr. Pike and explained I did have another meeting to attend. I proceeded to talk about advertisement and he agreed to a full page, which of course, I was quite happy. I scheduled another meeting to go over the advertisement and I thanked him again and left his office.
As I continued to work for the newspaper, I ran into an old friend of mine. I remembered how her daughter was murdered in our old junior high school. For years, they searched for her killer and for years, she waited for some kind of justice. My friend asked if I would participate in organizing a group of people to help build

a park in the memory of her daughter. I thought it would be a great thing to do.

My position with Al Dia was going along well until Mr. Pike offered me the position as his Public Relations Officer and offered me more money. Wow, I thought this would be great because I would have more money in my pocket and I could help more at home.

I was sad when I left the newspaper because I very much enjoyed working with Herman. As I said earlier in my experience, Herman was a great, modest and humble man. I am thankful to him for giving me the opportunity to work with him.

My position with the pharmacies did not start until my vehicle was finished being repaired. My girlfriend had invited me to attend a barbeque that was being given in the honor of her daughter; it was also a fundraiser and the event was held at the park where most of the people in North Camden attended. Pyne Point Park was a place where everyone went. People played handball, basketball and enjoyed swimming. I always thought it was a nice park. The memorial was perfect and it was such a beautiful day. There was dancing, food, music and games. To my surprise, the event had a dunking tank and Council President Milton Moran was the one being dunked. Wow! Moran did not have any problem in being dunked and he was a great sport about it.

I met several council members including Angel Fontez, President of the Board of Education, Gus Sennett.

The event was just great and everyone was having such a great time. During the event, awards were handed out and I just had a great feeling about the neighborhood coming together for such a positive and sad event because of the death of this young girl. My girlfriend Lane introduced me to Gus Sennett and at first; I did not care too much him. I thought he was just a little rough around the edges. We just shook hands and that was the end of our conversation.

The time was getting by me especially that I was having a good time and I knew that I would need a ride back to Philadelphia. Lane's friend offered me a ride home. I felt safe because this gentleman was a Camden Police Officer, so I did not give it much thought. I introduced Mark to my friend Lane and the Camden Officer. Mark was very nice to them and I was so happy that there was no tension. At times, Mark could be very standoffish if he didn't know you, but I know it did help that this man was a police officer also and was I ever thankful.

A few weeks later, Lane was having a small barbecue at home for the members of the Park Committee and Lane asked if I would like to attend. I said, "Sure why not?"
As Mark continued to move up in rank and had many more responsibilities that came with the position, I allowed myself to feel my position in my career was less important than Mark's. How I think about it now, Mark would often say that I was jealous of him. I remember that with every career move Mark made, I felt like it was happening to me. I was so proud of Mark. Mark had an image to uphold and the children and I lied more and more to protect his career, no matter what the cost was. The black eyes, the marks on my body, I would lie. I would constantly tell my family and friends that I had dropped a weight on my face or that I did something else, anything else.

Throughout the years, the abuse continued and I became so accustomed to the hitting. It was like changing my jeans. It was just another day in the Stun Family.

Many people thought that we were the perfect family and that nothing was wrong. I cried so many times, about how we had convinced people into believing how perfect our life was with Mark. It was just perfect. I was living a lie.

For many years, I allowed my husband and many other people to convince me that I was not worth a cent or that I could not accomplish anything in life. Then, it finally hit, me no one can make you feel bad about yourself but you. Years and years had gone by and the anger I felt towards myself was unbelievable. I had such low self-esteem at times. When I would call Daisy she would answer her phone, "Who is this?" I would say no one important and her response would be "Oh it's you Carmen." I tried to laugh it off, but I believe this always had a long and lasting effect on me.

The barbecue was very nice. It was just a handful of members; there was plenty of food and drinks to go around. We talked and joked about anything and everything. Our afternoon turned into the evening. There must have been just a few of us left and it was getting late. Lane put some soft, low music on so we could hear ourselves better. The members that were still there continued with the positive surroundings.

Gus Sennett attended the barbecue and as usual, I tried to ignore him. I must admit though, he had a great sense of humor, once you got to see a different side of him.

While I was trying to talk to the women and the other members at the gathering, Gus kept interrupting me. Like most men who want to be a part of the conversation, they act like little boys and you must give them your attention. So I thought I would be polite and I included him in our conversation.

Gus kidded around with me more and I did the same. When I think about it now, we all kidded around with each other. Gus wanted to know where I was from. I told him that I was born in Milwaukee, Wisconsin and my family came to Philadelphia, PA when I was three and we then moved to Camden, New Jersey when I was 12. Then I remembered who he was and I let him have it, I told him I was Daniel's aunt and that my husband had reached out to him about getting help. I told him what I thought about that horrible coach. Gus wanted to know why we didn't contact him and I said, "We did". Sadly, no help from your staff or from the school district we were not able to accomplish what we needed to help Daniel. I felt it was best to drop the topic because I knew how sensitive I was about the horrible treatment I received. Everyone finally realized it was time to go home and we were all saying our good-byes. I was on my cell phone calling Mark to tell him that I would be home soon. As I was hanging up the phone, Gus pulled up beside my vehicle. He asked me if I was OK and I said, "of course I am okay, I am calling my husband to let him know I am on my way home". I guess Gus was being a gentleman and making sure that the ladies were safe.

I began to tell Gus a little about my history here in Camden such as when my brother Arturo was killed. We were in city council constantly trying to get that horrible bar where my brother was killed closed down. We protested and we even brought our sleeping bags because we were planning on sleeping in city council chambers until they closed down that bar. I happen to be one of the original members of CCNC (Concerned Citizen's of North Camden). I was proud of myself. I marched in Washington, DC for equal rights; I volunteered my time for my community. I felt we needed a change back then and I still feel we need a positive change today.

A week after the gathering, I started my new position with Northgate and Westfield Pharmacy as their new Public Relations Officer. At first, I was real nervous as I was being introduced to the women from Northgate Pharmacy. Most of the ladies were quite nice and I realize that some were trying to figure me out. Back then, I did not understand why. As my time with the pharmacy moved on I understood why the ladies felt this way.

Then I arrived at Westfield Pharmacy and all of the women there were just as nice. I knew Leo from the old neighborhood and I knew Yeni and the other girls. As I was sitting at my desk it finally hit me, most of the women in the pharmacy were all Hispanic women and attractive women. The rumor and the gossip that went around the pharmacy was that Mr. Pike was a ladies' man. I could not stand for the nonsense or office gossip, so I ignored all the nonsense.

Mr. Pike was an average looking man. I always felt many of the women he was involved with were just interested in his money. Mr. Pike had several businesses. He did quite well for himself and my only concern was to do a great job for him as his Public Relations Officer, period.

Mr. Pike informed me that Mark and I were invited to attend a Good Will Banquet. Because I was Mr. Pike's representative, it was expected that I be there. For the first in my career, it was my time. My position was important. I was representing the Pharmacies and Mr. Pike. I was their representative. Maybe Mark was not used to me getting the attention; most of the time I was the one who had to sit back quietly. Don't get me wrong because I was so proud of Mark, but now I was the accomplished one and I felt great about it.

My husband did not like Mr. Pike! He felt he was too full of himself. Mr. Pike talked about his money and all the material things that money could buy.

At our Good Will Dinner, we honored Mr. Pike with a plaque for his generosity and donations to the company. My husband was not a happy camper and Mark did not care if anyone knew how unhappy he was with the event.

At the time, I was at a loss for words. Now, I look back at the time and laugh. It was truly amazing to me how much Mark and Mr. Pike were so much alike. No, we did not have money, but these two men were so full of themselves. How arrogant men can be and how some men think they are the last Coca Cola on the beach. Sadly, Mark's ugly side would come and the memory of his grandmother would show. There were so many times that it was difficult to be with my husband. God, how I loved this man but I continued to question his love for me.

Working for the Pharmacy was a happy time. Because of all these wonderful women that I met, I felt blessed. There was one in particular who would become one of my dearest and loving friends. Yeni is like my sister. The respect and love that I received will always be with me. I know this is what kept me strong when I deserved better in my life.

After the anger my husband expressed at the dinner I realize this was a business and I would have to separate my business life from my personal life.

Mr. Pike had informed me that he had given a $10,000 donation to the voter registration drive and I was scheduled to meet with Israel Envies to discuss a press conference. Mr. Pike wanted to inform the community of Camden that he had donated this money.

Now remember Mr. Pike was a proud man and it was quite important to him just as it was when he received all the plaques and trophies that he wanted recognition from Mr. Moran and Mr. Envies.

After many phone calls and missing each other, I was able to schedule a meeting with Mr. Envies. He was in charge of Congress for the Latino Community and at first I thought, "How nice".

He did not have me waiting long. As I sat in his office, I could not help but notice the painting and the atmosphere in the room. There was a huge painting of him and his wife. We chatted for a bit and then I got down to business. I was there to arrange a press conference that Mr. Pike had requested so the community would be aware of the large donations that he had given. Mr. Envies sat back in his chair and he looked at me trying to be smooth. I waited patiently for his next response. Mr. Envies did not want the press conference, nor did President of City Council Moran. Mr. Envies exact words were, "Mrs. Stun, we do not want the African American community to know that we received this large donation."

The color of my face must have turned pale white and I felt so sick to my stomach. Mr. Envies next words were, "If they know we have the money, they will want some of it". I was angry; the experience I endured with my husband's family was bad enough, but one of my own? How can we continue to treat each other in such a way? We must unite as a people and this man was worried about money and not wanting to share with the African American Community.

The political nightmare, this city was in for a surprise. How so many people trusted and respected these men. I knew that things were going to get worse and I was trying to stay completely out of it. I was not a registered voter in New Jersey. I was registered in Philadelphia, PA., where I lived.

I often wondered if Mr. Envies gave it any thought to who I was or who my husband was. Mark was African American and my daughter was half-black; maybe he could care less. My opinion of Mr. Envies was not so great. He was in denial about his African heritage; African blood runs through our veins. This experience with Mr. Envies showed me the community of Camden, New Jersey was in for the ride of their life and I knew that there was more to come. What was in store exactly, I didn't know. I just quietly waited for the next storm.

As I returned to my office and I sat down with Mr. Pike I informed him that Mr. Envies and Mr. Moran did not want a press conference and I expressed to him the exact words that Mr. Envies repeated to me.

We sat there silently and I am sure many things went through Mr. Pike's mind, but he never expressed his feelings to me and our meeting was over.

From this day on, I observed and watched all the political nonsense that took place in the City of Camden. Many mayor's and council people have come and gone, and have completely forgotten who they worked for. They worked for the people of the City of Camden, New Jersey. The voters are what put them in office and so many have completely forgotten whom they were supposed to help.

Work continued as always, we prepared for health fairs and advertisements with the Spanish radio and preparing for St. John the Baptist Parade. Mr. Pike and I attended Democratic Committee meetings and so many other functions concerning the political nonsense in the City.

One afternoon I received a phone call from Gus Sennett. I thought this would be a great meeting with the President of the Board Of Education. Gus and I could go over some ideas about our pharmacy and discuss what we could provide for the schools. Our meeting was scheduled for the following afternoon. Then the meeting was re-scheduled and happy because truthfully I was not prepared. This gave me plenty of time to present a proposal to Mr. Sennett, which I was quite happy to do.

The following late afternoon, as I was preparing to go home, I received a phone call from Mr. Sennett and he wondered if it was possible if we could have dinner, now of course I did not give it much thought because this was a business meeting, I thought, so I agreed.

As I was waiting at the pharmacy parking lot, Mr. Sennett arrived and he asked if I would like to take one car. Curiously, it did not make much sense to me, but I was mainly concerned with getting business from the school district, so I once again, I agreed.

As we arrived at the restaurant and we were both seated. Mr. Sennett ordered a drink and then I started to realize our surroundings. It was not exactly what I had expected. I can laugh about it now but this was not a business meeting. The atmosphere was very romantic, there were candles lit up everywhere and Gus began to tell me about his family history. He told me that his father was once the City Council President for the Camden, New Jersey. He told me how his father had died of a stroke.

I quietly sat and I thought to myself, maybe he's making small talk and anytime now we were talk about the Pharmacies and what we can provided. Just as I was about to speak, Mr. Sennett offered me a piece of Italian bread with peppers and shoved it into my mouth. My alarms went off. Mr. Sennett, I said, "Are you coming on to me, or is this a business meeting?"

Gus admitted that he was flirting with me. I would be a liar if I did not say I found him to be very attractive, but I also thought this man has a very strong personality. Whom am I kidding; I thought he was loud and sometimes rude.

I would be a liar if I said I was not flattered. Gus was in a relationship and I was married. My marriage has not been right for so long and there is no excuse.

Yes my affair with Gus was very short and sweet. Gus's girlfriend called my home and told Mark that I was bothering her boyfriend. Funny, when I think about it now, but this woman was "special". I refuse to attack anyone's character and I could only give her my utmost respect. No one deserves to be treated like nothing, and Gus and I just caused hurt and pain to two people we were supposed to have loved.

Of course my marriage became worse than ever and many times after work I would stop by and see my friend Lane. I just did not want to go home. Mark was angry, I was sad, and no matter how hard we tried. The abuse I sustained over the years was so overwhelming and my affairs did not help matters.

A new election was coming up and many people in the Latino community wanted three different candidates to run for the new Mayor of the city of Camden. There was, of course, President of City Council Moran, School Board Member Mr. Dale, and City Councilmen Fontez. The Latino communities arranged special forums and I did not want any part of this ridiculous campaign. At times, I would voice my concerns; I would say, "Do you realize you are dividing the Latino community?" No one really cared to hear what I had to say.

Mr. Pike insisted upon my attendance at several of the forums and he felt it was important that I did exactly as he requested. I did not give any opinion in regard to any of this nonsense. Mr. Dale asked if I would have lunch with him and I agreed. As Public Relations Officer for Mr. Pike, I was able to communicate better with most people. Mr. Pike was the moneyman. They knew he was the one to go to for contributions for their campaign. My secret support for Mayor was and always will be Angel Fontez. Angel cared about the people of Camden and he wanted to do so much to help the city.

I tried to stay away and out of this special campaign but for some reason they felt I should be involved because I was the representative for Mr. Pike. Sadly, I thought it was all crazy, but this is what Mr. Pike wanted.

Many of the forums would make my head spin. I would say to myself, "Are these men out of their minds, or do they give a damn about this city?" One afternoon Gus called me during the special election. He asked if I could arrange a special meeting with Mr. Pike. I asked him, "May I ask what it is in regards to?" He told me that Mr. Sennett also wanted to run for Mayor and he wanted the support and funds from Mr. Pike. I could not believe what I had just heard and my head began to start spinning again. I politely said, "I will try to arrange a meeting and I will get back to you".

Mr. Pike agreed to meet with Gus. Leo, Mr. Pike and I were all present at the meeting. Gus gave a great presentation and we all believed he could have been a great mayor but things did not turn out the way he had hoped.
Sadly, Milton Moran won the special election and I felt strongly about the person who should be the first Latino Mayor for the City of Camden. We needed a positive mayor for the entire community of people in Camden, New Jersey. Did the community realize they had selected the wrong person for Mayor of the City of

Camden? I felt Angel Fontez would have been a better mayor.

Angel and I spoke and I expressed how I felt. Angel, "I cannot express it in public because of my position with the pharmacy but please let me say this to you, "I know you would have been the better person for this city."

Finally, things went back to normal and I had other things to attend to. There was the banquet for the Hispanic Police Officers. We all joined in helping the Halloween Banquet for the Park Committee. We did not get as many people as we had hoped but we were all thankful.

Not long after the Halloween Banquet, the park committee folded and everyone went his or her own way. No one it seemed could come to an agreement.

During the Christmas holidays, Mr. Pike donated toys for the children in the area and I was quite busy with dropping off the toys and arranging the Christmas dinner for all the ladies from both Pharmacies. Mr. Pike wanted all the women from both pharmacies to get along better. I think some of the women butted heads a lot when phone calls were exchanged. Our Christmas dinner was a great success and I was extremely happy.

I am sure you may be wondering when the abuse was taking place in my marriage because I was not home very much anymore. Due to my position as Public Relations Officer and Mark being busy with his position on the police department, the children were older so there was much more distance between us and we both realized it more than ever.

Mark and I had a special nightclub that we use to go to called Brazil. So many times I felt like an outsider. Mark's friends were other police officers, FBI agents and so on. One particular time, which will always stay with me, was when all his buddies were with him and he sat me in our usual corner. Mark stepped away and a man came and sat next to me and he began to chat with me and asked me to dance; of course, I said, "No." But, he asked why and I expressed to the man that I was not here alone. He then asked me, "Who are you with?" I said, "I'm here with my husband." He looked around and said, "Where is your husband?" I pointed to Mark and his buddies and said, "Right over there."

Mark and his buddies would call themselves the" Rat Pack." I would watch how they acted like proud peacocks and they thought they were kings of something. No one would come near the small corner of the club.

The New Year's before my surgery I remember I asked Mark if we could do something else. I asked if we could just spend some special time with each other but this was out of the question.

Mark and his Rat Pack started hanging out at a nightclub in New York City. No girlfriends or wives were allowed. I knew something was going on but I did what Mark was doing, I watched and observed. For years, I questioned whether my husband truly loved me. I guess it didn't matter anymore if he still loved me, I could tell that he didn't. I knew there was something going on, but did not have the proof!

As the months continued forward and Valentine's Day was approaching, this is when the pharmacies did well economically. I decided that through flyers and advertisement, we could do so much better, and we did. I went around all four corners of the city; did I ever hustle. Mr. Pike was so pleased with the outcome for Valentine's Day.

The next day as Yeni, I, and the rest of the staff were trying to recuperate from Valentine's Day, I was sitting at my desk when Mr. Pike called me over the intercom and requested that I come to the top floor. To my surprise, Mr. Moran and his aid Douglass Bradley were waiting to speak to me. I was informed that I would be working on Mr. Moran's Campaign for Mayor. The expression on my face must have told them exactly how I felt. I was not prepared for this at all and the next words that came out of my mouth must have surprised them. I said, "I am not a registered voter here in Camden; I am a registered voter from Philadelphia. Why would you want me to work on your campaign?"

Mr. Moran expressed to me that he felt that I would be a great asset to the campaign and felt that I had a gift with people. This was utter bull. After Mr. Moran and Doug left the office, Mr. Pike and I entered his office and I said, "Mr. Pike why does this man want me to work on his campaign?" He could not answer my question. I reasoned that they wanted me as the go between to Mr. Pike and Mr. Moran as well as the money that Mr. Pike could donate to the campaign.

From February until Election Day, I would have to go to the pharmacies to see what was needed of me then I would go to the Main Campaign Headquarters. My stress level was so high and this had a major affect on my health. Mr. Moran would ask me to attend campaign walks through the neighborhood. I was even responsible for decorating several headquarters. I would often think and say to myself, "Is this really happening?" I did exactly what I was told and I made it a point to keep my mouth shut and my eyes open.

I felt one of the most positive things occurring was that Ms. Dorothy Jones and Ms. Maggie Rhodes were running on the same ticket with Mr. Moran, but what truly scared me was the Mr. Envies was also on the same ticket. I knew his true feelings were against African Americans and it made my insides turn.

One afternoon and I was coming into the main headquarters, I was just about to take my first step up the stairs when Mr. Moran asked me if I could accompany him. I said "Milton, where is Dan?" But no, he wanted me to attend. I wanted to know where we were going and he would not completely answer my question. Dan did not look very happy and I was a bit confused.

As I sat in his car, I continued to think to myself, "Where in the hell are we going?" I have to admit, it did scare me because no one knew where I was except Mr. Moran. When we finally arrived to our destination this is when I realized we were at a Country Club. My first thought was, "Why are we here and why is my presence necessary at this Country Club?" I was introduced to two very pleasant men, and as I recall, one of the men's name was Mr. Lee.
Mr. Lee and I made small talk. I spoke of who my husband was. I also told him where I grew up in Philadelphia and where I was baptized, which happened to be our largest Catholic parish in the city. Mr. Wong was also from the same parish and he spoke of how well he knew Chief Inspector Woh. I knew of Chief Inspector Woh and it was all positive, nothing negative.

As Mr. Lee and I continued talking, Mr. Moran and the other gentlemen were in a very private conversation, I was not able to hear what was taking place.

After lunch, we all attended a meeting with the owner of a very large Architect Company. I was not formally introduced. I remember shaking his hand but I just do not remember his name.

I was very much impressed with the company. Their company was a block long and it was a very old building. I was seated in one of the offices and all four men disappeared into another office and spider senses were saying "what in the heck is going on and who is this man"?

As the campaign continued forward, something was just not right and out of the clear blue, Mr. Envies felt he had to leave the main headquarters. Mr. Envies gave no reason or explanation, he just left. My spider senses and women's intuition was running on high but all I could do was watch and listen. An awful smell was starting to arise at the campaign headquarters and it was beginning to scare me to no end. I became so consumed with the pharmacies and with this horrible campaign that I overlooked what was taking place in my home.

I knew Mark was involved with someone and I could not prove it. Therefore, I just went along with the program. One thing I learned from my husband was to always be observant of people and their behavior. Because of my training through Mark, I made sure I did exactly what I learned from him.

One afternoon Mr. Pike called me and asks me to pick up a check for Mr. Envies. There goes my spider senses; I could not understand why Mr. Envies needed this money. I knew for a fact that Mr. Pike was giving a large amount of contributions to the campaign.

When I picked up the check and Mr. Pike did not put it in an envelope, I could not help but to take a peek at the check. The check was made out to the Israel Dork Campaign. Ding, Ding, Ding, my warning signals just hit a major high. Slowly I drove to Mr. Envies home and handed the check to his wife. It was best not to have a long conversation with her and I politely excused myself and explained that I was very busy. Next, I extended my goodbyes.

As I arrived at the headquarters and I entered Mr. Moran's office I did not hesitate to ask Mr. Moran, "Why did Mr. Envies have his own personal campaign and why did he need this money"? Mr. Moran just gave me a blank look and it hit me like ton of bricks, the little voice in my head said, "LEAVE RIGHT NOW!"

I became quite ill and I began having chest pains; I felt numbness in my left arm. My sister Marcia was the receptionist at the main headquarters and she was the one who called the ambulance.

One of the other workers did not feel it was best to wait for the ambulance and she was kind enough to rush me over to Cooper Medical Center.

I asked Marcia to call Mark. When Mark arrived, he was just annoyed that he had to rush over to the hospital.

Sadly, I was admitted into the hospital for two days for observation and test. It was not a heart attack nor was it a stroke; I was under a lot of stress and everything became unbearable. I was aware of some ugly campaigning. Mr. Moran and Mr. Envies were getting ready to turn their backs on two wonderful women who deserved the position as council people.

I took a week off to get my nervous system back in order and in no time, I was back at work and back with this horrible campaign. As time continued and I finally realized why Mr. Envies left the main headquarters. This horrible man was helping another man to run for city council, which took the votes away from Dorothy and Maggie.

Ms. Jones and Ms. Reed were just two African American women on the same ticket as Mr. Moran and Mr. Envies but they were not meant to win along with Moran and Dork. Because of the dirty dealing which had taken place; the votes were split.

Moran and Envies won the campaign and these two wonderful women lost. How sad this is, all this time these two wonderful women were used as a token for the campaign. Neither Milton nor Envies cared what they did to Dorothy and Maggie. These two wonderful women wanted to do so much for the people of city Camden, New Jersey.

When the final results came out most of the people who thought they were supporting the right men for the position as Mayor and city council were all numb and we could not understand or believe how in the hell this could have happened or understand why they would be low down and dirty. My disgust over this would not allow me to celebrate and I knew helping these two men win the election was like helping to put the devil and one of his demons into office.

Mr. Moran and Mr. Envies and several other people were all celebrating and everyone kept asking if I was heading out to Puerto Rico and I had no idea what they were talking about, I made it quite clear and to the point that I had no intentions of going anywhere. My plans were to continue as Public Relations Officer for the Pharmacies and nothing else.

My inner spirit would not allow me to stay any further and quietly I got into my car and drove back to Philadelphia. During my drive back, I did a lot of soul searching and deep down in my gut, the horrible feeling took over me and my inner soul said, "Dear God what just took place?" I walked into my home and I began to tell Mark what had happened. Mark made it clear to me that he never liked Moran and he knew there was more to this man than meets the eye.

The next morning I woke up to a new day in which this horrible campaign was over. I did not have to deal with it any further and when I arrived at the pharmacy, I felt everything would be back to normal. Then Mr. Pike called me into his office. He informed me that he wanted to give a dinner in honor of the new Mayor, Milton Moran. Goodness, I was at a loss for words.

With the help of Yeni, we were able to plan a wonderful dinner for Moran. I just refused to invite that idiot Dork and I might have bitten too much but at this point, I had enough of the political horror that was taking place. Mr. Envies and I had words earlier that week and I made it clear that I was not afraid. I expressed myself to Mr. Envies, I knew what a racist pig he is and how so many African Americans had voted for him that he should be ashamed of himself. I realized this might cost me my position with the pharmacy but I did not care.
Mr. Pike was very pleased with the outcome of the dinner and the way Yeni and I arranged everything. Then it finally dawned on me that the only thing my husbanded ever attended with me was the St. John the Baptist Banquet. During the dinner's and functions, I just didn't feel close to Mark, but no matter how deep I sunk into my hole, the love I felt never left me. I prayed to God to please help me.

The dinner came and went and I prayed that our relationship would have been better; I portrayed a woman with a perfect marriage. It was great and the image that my husband needed to uphold had to be perfect. Knowing quite well deep down inside it was all a lie.

I was in California when Mark received the great news that he was runner up for the George Fecal Award and I was so happy for him, but I knew something more was going on at home. My daughter Elizabeth called me and informed me that her dad, my husband, was receiving phone calls from this woman and each time she tried to get the number her dad would delete it from the caller ID.

Elizabeth begged me not to tell her father what she told me and I promised my daughter that I would never disclosed what she said to me. For two years, I watched my husband and his behavior. The night I returned from California, I knew deep in my soul my husband was having an affair. Even when he touched me, I could tell. Our love was over and something deep in my soul knew the abuse was going to get worse.

Mark came in second in the George Fecal award. Stupid me made a comment that maybe his sister should not attend because she was in the process of going into Federal prison for embezzlement from the two NFL players. What does he do; he excluded our sons Samuel and Manuel. I am ashamed of how he treated the boys.

They were so proud of him, but he was not proud of them. "How dare you!" I would think to myself, "Your sister is a crook protected by you and your mother and you make justification for her illegal bullshit." I knew right then and there, my husband did not truly love our sons as a father should love their sons.

Mr. Pike gave me my notice, and it was a relief; I knew too much. I was exhausted with all the political crap and Mark thought that it would have been a great idea if I took a trip to California to visit my girlfriend Lora and her husband Bruce. So, I took him up on his offer and I made the trip to California. I realize the only reason Mark wanted me out of the house was because he was busy with his new love.

It was great seeing them again and I called home to see how things were going. Mark said everything was just great but what he did not know was Elizabeth told me that he would get up in the middle of the night and leave our home after he received a phone call on his cell. He was also receiving phone calls at the house from this woman. Elizabeth tried several times to get a glimpse of the woman's first name; it was Dee.

I did the next best thing; I watched and observed Mark for two years. His idiot buddies would try to convince me my husband was a good boy and I would look at them and in my mind I would say, "Why are you idiots trying so hard to convince me?" I already knew what was going on with my husband and Dee.

The Code of Silence was always there. Wives, girlfriends, lovers and so on do not exist with the city police, state police or any law enforcement. We were second-class citizens or at least so they thought!

The night that I returned from California will be a night that I will never forget. Before I returned, Lora and I stopped by Victoria Secret and I bought this beautiful nightgown. I hoped maybe this would bring some kind of spark that was missing back to our lives. I was picked up from the airport and it was great to see Mark. I went upstairs and got into the shower; lotion, perfumed and put on the nightgown. When I came out of the bathroom, my husband got one look at me and said, "I CAN SEE THROUGH IT." I could not believe my ears! I thought that was the purpose of the nightgown. It confirmed my heart that my husband was having an affair. Our marriage was over.

One night Mark received a distress phone call from "Little Man." Little Man stated one of his old girlfriends had showed up at his house and he could not get rid of her. What a crock! I knew Mark was meeting with Dee because that son of a bitch did not come back home until 5:30am.

Thank you "Little Man"; thank you for calling me out of character the night we were all at Red Lobster and never apologizing for calling me a whore in Spanish. Thank you Mark for not being the man I fell in love with so many years ago and not defending me, my knight in shining armor. I felt my inner soul vanish away by not being able to help myself.
As time went on, I continued to watch my husband's behavior. My horrible nightmares became worse. I could see the women in my dreams but I could never see her face. I would wake up crying and screaming. Mark would say that I was crazy; but one particular night he said as I was having the reacquiring dream again and he "saw a dark shadow looming over our bed." I would say to Mark, I know the woman is short with dark hair but I cannot see her face, and this dream would haunt me for two years.

A huge article was printed in the Philadelphia Daily Newspaper. Evelyn Howard from Channel 10 News interviewed Mark. Ms. Howard was a classy woman and left a good impression on me.

Mark changed so much it was no longer us. It was only him and our family was not important to him anymore; I knew that our marriage was over.

My cousin Bret was married on New Year's Eve, not long after the award ceremony. I could tell that he did not want to be there with me but we went through the motions. Even after we left the reception and arrived at the nightclub, the sadness was so obvious that in lingered in the air between us.

Mark was now waiting to make police Inspector. As his wife, I thought maybe I just wasn't doing everything in my power to give positive support to my husband. Commissioner Nate did not like my husband and there was a constant battle between them. Mark was not promoted to Inspector because of Commissioner Nate. Eventually though, Mark did get promoted to Inspector.

A month or so after his promotion to I started attending classes because my dream was to become a writer. From the very beginning of our marriage, this is all I wanted to do. I wanted to write about my experiences as a child and about how I survived the drug abuse that I witnessed.

Mark was honored by business people in the 17th District. There were many politicians there including our Mayor; I remember it like it was yesterday. Mark thanked the children and me for supporting him all these years as he moved up in ranks in the Philadelphia Police Department. We protected Mark through the years. We kept the code of silence. This is the only reason why Mark moved up through the ranks!

One of the most important comments I would repeat to my children was it did not matter where you came from or what language you speak. You can be anything you want to be in life. Mark said "Hey its fine. You go back to school. My salary is really good and you don't have to worry about working until you've completed school." I took his word as a man and as my husband.

While I attended classes I continued to clean, cook and paint everything that was necessary to keep the house the way we both wanted it. Mark never had to worry about anything. I thought maybe if I did the painting and other odd jobs around the house he would not have to worry about the up keep on the house. How hard I tried to please him.

So many times, I would feel so guilty. Mark would get angry about the food bill and I tried to buy the minimum. Even when I wanted new furniture, I felt guilty when I asked for anything. Mark said we could not afford it and I respected his decisions. Mark's grandmother gave us her old dining room table and I realized that it needed some work so I felt that the best thing to do was to strip and redo it so that Mark did not have to worry about buying new furniture.

Mark was kind enough to agree to a new kitchen during the time I was working on my project with the dining room table, I took my time striping the table; I knew that it was going to take me some time to complete this complex job but I would do it.

The job took three months to finish. One afternoon as I was sanding the table Mark arrived from home, when he came into the door he seemed upset and I asked him if he was okay? Of course, I knew something was not right but I asked anyway, I could not believe the words I heard from my husband's mouth; he proceeded to call me every name in the book; whore, bitch, and slut and so on. Elizabeth, our daughter, was in her bedroom listening to her father. Foolish me being strong minded and never holding my tongue, I yelled back at him and I said, "I don't know where you've been or who you've been with, but I want you to turn back around and take that shit right back to the bitch you were with!"

This was a horrible mistake because with that the next thing I remember was that Mark came from the living room into the dining room and hit me so hard across the face that I saw a flash of light in front of my eyes. Dear God, I knew something terrible had just happened to my eye.

Many times during the abuse, I would say to Mark, "One day you are going to hit me and you are going to cause me severe damage and it will not be reversible."

We started struggling and he had me in the corner of the kitchen with his hands around my throat. I was trying to fight him with every ounce of my being. I knew right then and there Mark wanted to kill me and I felt it. Poor Elizabeth, she ran down the stairs and into the kitchen and jumped on her father's side pulling at his arm so he would let me go.

Every time Mark would hit me, he would say, "If you report this to the Police, I am going to lose my job and get locked up. What will happen to you and the kids?"

Where do I get my Courage? Where do I get my strength? Where do I get my determination? GOD!!!

I refuse to hide. I refuse to keep silent. My voice and my book will help others who have been afraid, my voice and my book will help many come out of that dark hole.

I do not feel pity for myself; I am a strong, positive and determined woman. I realized some time ago, coming out and speaking against Domestic Violence involving police officers would strike a nerve.

Many of us have not survived, many will live with scars but…..Many of us will speak out.

To those who are uncomfortable with my book, I pray that you will find it in your heart to show compassion to the women, children and men who are victims and survivors of Domestic Violence.

My courage is what keeps me going and because of the GREAT SPIRIT. I WILL CONTINUE TO SPEAK OUT!

The final assault came when I called Mark's buddy Edwin Castro and I begged him to please come and get Mark out of the house just for a bit; but Mark refused to leave. Mark even refused to talk to Edwin over the phone. Edwin said he knew he was beating me but what could he do, Mark was his boss. Many people knew Mark had put his hands on me many times, but everyone looked the other way.

The week of the abuse, I was preparing to attend one of my oldest friend's wedding and I had bruises on my neck and chest. Sadly, the dress that I was planning to wear could not cover the bruises. I felt so terrible because I wanted so much to attend the wedding.

No makeup would cover up my bruises. Edwin said, "Wear a turtleneck. It was very warm that day so Mark made up an excuse that I was home sick in bed. Yes, I was sick; the depression from the recent abuse was just too much."

The months continued to go by and my depression worsened with each moment, I knew without second-guessing that something was wrong with my vision. I was too afraid to go to the doctors. God, I just knew. The holidays came and went and my depression just consumed me.

One afternoon, I remember telling Mark that there was something wrong with my eye. He had nothing to say. The usual holidays at home continued and I was nice enough to hold a baby shower for my sister-in-law Delia for her fifth child. During the shower, my heart was so heavy because I was aware of how bad my vision had become; I was beside myself.

Before I go any further, I am sure many wonder why I did not call the police. He is the police, he was now Inspector for the Philadelphia Police Department and his word was gold. Mark was the golden child of the Philadelphia Police Department and they would have covered this up. Just like many other cases of Violence by Police Officers.

I continued with classes and more withdrawn and very quiet, Mark was not aware or could care less because he was so wrapped up in his new friend and himself. Mark would arrive at home and he would tell me what took place at work during the day. I would listen and continue my so called wifely duties, made dinner, served dinner and always gave my undivided attention to the master, as he would call himself.

One afternoon when Doris was visiting she became aware that I was attending classes. Doris would say, "What about Mark?" I never tried to discourage Mark and I always supported my husband in anything he wanted to do in his career. I often would say to Mark, "Love, if you want to go back to school, I am here for you". I often wondered if my mother-in-law knew how many times I encouraged her son to go back to school. I truly believe Mark never took the time to tell his mother the truth, or maybe he did, I will never know.

Daisy's brother Mathew was getting married and she needed my help. I was more than happy to help with the wedding arrangements. Daisy, her sister-in-law to be Heather and I, and, went shopping for her wedding dress. I was flattered because they needed my help and it took my mind away from home. Daisy arranged a small bridal shower for Heather.

The bridal shower was quite small; it was Daisy, Mary, Heather and I. I was the designated driver and we were having such a wonderful time until then the floaters in my vision became worse. When I arrived home, I told Mark I was going to schedule an appointment with the doctor and he was not concerned nor did he make a comment about it.

When I arrived at Dr. Rodriquez and I was seated, I explained to him the problem with my right eye. I was experiencing a lot of flashes and something was floating in my eye. I described to Dr. Rodriquez there appeared to be "snakes" squiggling around in front of my vision. Dr. Rodriquez looked into my eyes and he explained he was not a specialist but if the symptoms continued, to call him.

At that end of the week as I was driving to my OB/GYN's office, nothing was fine because I continued to have floaters and flashes. On my way driving back home, I could not believe what happened next, I noticed a dark shadow taking over my vision and I thought to myself, "OH GOD, what's wrong with my eye?" I was completely freaking out, my brain was racing a million miles a minute and I would pray to God to just please let me make it back home in one piece.

The fear of hitting someone with my car frighten me unbelievably I felt I was losing control and I kept praying. I drove directly to the Dr. Rodriquez and he did a quick exam. Dr. Rodriguez sent me directly to the Eye Specialist that was located not far from his office. Even as the dark shadow continued to take over my vision, I got right back into the car and drove myself to the Eye Specialist.

I was seen right away and there were several doctors' who were examining me, one doctor asked me if I had been hit recently and I lied. I remembered so well how this happened and I waited patiently as the doctors continued to examine me. They even performed an ultra sound on my right eye. When the exam was over and the entire tests were complete, five doctors were in my room and finally the news came out. I had retinal detachment from the right eye and I would need surgery.

I broke down; I cried hysterically because I knew my vision would never be the same. I was not a doctor but my heart and soul knew the outcome was not going to be good. These wonderful doctors tried everything to calm me down. Right away, I said, "I need to call my husband". When I was able to get Mark on the phone, he seemed quite angry that I was disturbing him. I knew what a busy man he was but I needed his help and compassion. This horrible man knew he was the cause of my retinal detachment.

Finally, it happened, my silence cost me my right eye and the man who did this to me did not want any part of me or the responsibility for the horrible abuse I had sustained from him year after year. My retina detached in two separate places. I knew right then and there that my heart would never heal from this.
My heart ached with so much pain I could not believe this was happening to me. I never blamed God for the abuse or questioned why. All I could do was pray for compassion and strength.

The doctor's first tried to schedule the surgery at a different hospital but there was no room for me. Then the surgery was scheduled to take place at the Eye Hospital. We arrived at the hospital and Mark was still annoyed and angry. All I could do was cry; Mark showed no emotion, no compassion, nothing.

The doctor from the Will's Eye Institute examined my right eye again and asked the same question the other doctors asked, "DID SOMEONE HIT YOU OR DID YOU FALL?" I said, "No one hit me nor did I fall." The shame I felt right then and there, because I lied again to protect Inspector Stun.

My eye surgery was scheduled for the following morning and I was in so much distress all I could do was cry. I was feeling such emptiness from my husband. Mark showed no concern about my eye, nor did he show me compassion. I went into the surgery feeling alone and sad and awoke with this horrible sense of fear; even in my sleep I could feel the emptiness.

I awoke and my daughter Elizabeth and Mark were there. I could not see them but I could hear their voices. Mark was not himself and I knew something was wrong but I could not see his face. I went home and I could feel the coldness from Mark. He made sure that I got my drops put in my eye and continued through the motions of trying to help me but I knew we had come to the end of the road.

Mathew and Heather's Wedding reception was held at our home and I was up in bed with bandages on my eye. I tried so hard to make small talk with everyone but I was just not feeling up to it. Everyone showed concern except my husband. Everything went on as usual and Mark would take me to my eye doctor appointments after my surgery; and then he told me.

Mark told me right then and there at the doctor's office that he wanted to leave and I said, "Mark, my God, I just had surgery and you want to leave?" It did not matter to him and I know that we both lived a lie for so many years. The love was gone and in the end, the abuse cost me my right eye.

I must have not loved myself very much, I recall saying to this man who hurt me physically, mentally and emotionally so much that I would die for him. In return, I got nothing but pain, shame and guilt.

The morning that my husband left me, we made love for the first time since my surgery and that afternoon, I called Mark to tell him what I was preparing for dinner. Not long after our afternoon conversation, I received a phone call from Mark, "Carmen, I am not coming home nor am I coming back". I could not believe my ears but I knew that someday this was going to happen and I was heartbroken. What was I going to do? I knew I would not be able to drive again because I was not able to see. My right eye was irreversibly damaged and there were fibers still floating in my eye that the doctor's were not able to remove. I cried and cried and even with all that had happened with the abuse and the surgery, I still wanted my husband back. Was it because I loved him, was it because I knew that he already had someone else, what reason did I still want to be with this man that caused me so much pain. At this time in my life, I could not answer these questions.

The anger of abandonment and hurt took every bit of my soul; I just felt pain. Even after our separation, Mark still wanted to come around and have sex. I knew Dee was in the picture and I kept my promise to our daughter Elizabeth. I believe Mark felt having sex with two different women, did so much for his ego. Did I ever realize how much ego this man carried with him? I would receive phone calls from a little girl asking for her mother and she would say, "My mother is with her friend but it's a secret I can't tell you who my mother's friend is"; I could hear another woman on the other end of the receiver. Mark was out with Dee and whoever was babysitting this little girl was having this poor child call me.

I am sure many women have followed the character from the movie "Waiting to Exhale" when the husband left and he left all of his belongings behind. Mark left his belongings behind too. I had a "good-bye party." The surfboard Mark loved so much was gone, the suits I bought, gone, the sport jacket gone. Yes! ALL GONE; I destroyed it all.

One Monday afternoon I was served with divorce papers and on that Thursday, Mark came by to give me some money to help pay some of the bills. Mark still wanted to have sex with me and I could not believe it.

Now I know men like Mark enjoyed controlling and enjoying the power of control. I said to Mark "what, I am not good enough for you to stay married to but I'm good enough to have sex with?" Mark's response was, "Oh Carmen, you just look good". What a bunch of crap. I had enough of the threats and the calls and the mental and emotional abuse. I filed for an order for protection from abuse.

Everyone flipped. Mark said no one would listen to me, not even his Police Commissioner. The Police Commissioner's opinion of me was that I was crazy. Mark would just laugh at me; all I could do was cry. I allowed the abuse to go on in my life as well as the abuse my boys went through, and I lied repeatedly for my husband.

When Mark, me, and Elizabeth appeared in court, not only was my mother-in-law, father-in-law and Jezebel there, but also my old friend. Yes, my friend, the one that I thought was my friend, the one that my husband wanted to sleep with time and time again.

My daughter Elizabeth was seven months pregnant and they were all standing outside of the courthouse when her grandmother proceeded to argue with her, calling Elizabeth a liar. Elizabeth said to her grandmother, "I saw daddy hitting her and I am not going to lie for him." My mother-in-law made such a seen they had to bring Elizabeth into the building. Once Elizabeth was sitting next to me, she made it very clear to Mark's attorney she was not going to lie for him.

No one was allowed on the floor with me, not my daughter; but Mark's FBI friend John and his cop friends were all there. Was this an intimidation tactic? I was alone!

Not long after the court hearing my electricity, phone and gas was shut off. Mark had them all shut off and he refused to give me any money to pay for it and because everything was in his name. I was screwed. My mother financially helped me with my first attorney. I had nothing and my mother was there.

So, between my attorney and my husband's attorney, a motion was filed stating that in order for me to get any money, I would have to drop the order of abuse and again this man would have control. I gave up my rights to keep a roof over our head. The judge must have known, but what could I do, nothing. I had no money and I could not see like I use to out of my right eye. I felt as though someone just tore my independence away from me. I was no one; this was just the beginning of so much to come. After a brief meeting with the lawyers, Mark and I never spoke again.

Mark wanted me to sign the divorce papers right away and I refused. I knew I was entitled to something but what I did not know just then. I had no money, I was not working anymore, and mostly my vision was coming mainly from my left eye and I thanked God for what sight I did have. For sixteen years of my life, I lied and protected Mark so he would not lose his job but in the end, I lost so much more than he could ever imagine. Time and time again, I remember telling my husband to please stop hitting me in my face. No matter how much I begged, my cries were unheard.
Samantha Yolanda Hughes was born on January 28, 2000 and she was the angel that was sent to me. With all the sadness and emptiness I felt, Elizabeth and my son's were the most positive things in my life. I called

my mother to tell her about this angel GOD sent to me. I said, "Mami, she looks so much like him, my deceased brother." My mother and father came to the hospital where my granddaughter was born and when she held her, she cried because she saw the child that was taken from her so many years ago.

A month after Samantha was born, Angel passed away. I never lost contact with her. Angel meant so much to me and to find out about her death the way I did, will always be with me.
One afternoon I received a phone call from a friend and a Philadelphia Police Dispatcher, she said, "Carmen, did you hear. Hear what?" "Mark's grandmother died". I dropped the phone and my sobs of pain echoed through the house. Gloria apologized for upsetting me and I said, "No Gloria, thank you so much for calling me." Mark did not even want me or the children to attend the services. He made it quite clear; I was no longer a part of the family. No matter what he said, I remember very clearly what I said to her many years before she went home to God. I would always be there no matter what. The pain in my heart was unbelievable. This family knew how close Angel and I were.

They were trying to hide the abuse that their son did to me, they would rather I did not pay my last respects to this wonderful woman I was blessed to know.

Mark did not want me at the services and he did not hide his feelings. Dee was introduced to everyone as his girlfriend. My children were taken aback by all of this. I was still his wife and Mark was showing everyone at his grandmother's funeral services, that Dee, was now a part of the family and myself and the children were no longer a part of his family.

During holidays and special occasions, Mark would have our children meet him at Burger King and Home

Depot parking lots. Our oldest son Samuel finally expressed himself to his father and wanted to know if his dad ever regretted adopting him and brother. Mark said "NO" but Samuel found it so hard to believe him because of the way he continued to treat him and Manuel.

There was so much anger with my children, so much pain and no matter how hard I tried to keep the peace, to no avail the anger continued through my children and through the years. My son Manuel got himself into some trouble and he would always say, "Did dad leave because of me"? I would tell my son, "No son, dad has a new life and girlfriend and he was not happy here anymore". Mark would often say to our friends that, I was angry because he left, and I would say bullshit, "I knew our marriage was ending, what I am angry about is what he did to my eye and he left"! Never carrying about the end result of his abuse and what the lasting affect it had on my vision and the lasting emotional affect and physical affect. I was not able to drive anymore, I took risk by driving our car, I knew I could not see as well as I use to before the surgery. I was not willing to give up my independence.

Before my the abuse caused me to have retinal detachment, I am proud to say, that I was a jack-of-all-trades. From Receptionist, Administrative Assistant, Clerk Typist for a Law Firm, Fitness consultant, Sales/Writer for the Spanish Newspaper and my last position was Public Relations Officer.

With each position, I held pride and respect for myself. So, many nights after Mark left I would cry myself to sleep praying to God and asking what am I to do. I was afraid that our legal system was not going to help me at all. Several friends said I should apply with social security for SSI and I did just that and when I met with the Social Service Administrator and I told him what happen to my vision he was quite direct and to the point.

Mrs. Stun, if I were you and because your husband did this to you, you should go after him for spousal support. The income, SSI provides will not be enough and this is not fair to you.

So, I was examined by a state doctor and I remember when we arrived at his office building and I looked away quickly, I did not see the last step and I fell. I was angry, and I cried, I cried because this was not me, this was not the person I was anymore.

During the time, I waited patiently for my order of spousal support, there was so much drama taking place at home. When Mark left our home and not knowing if I was coming or going, I decided to go to counseling. Wow! What could I say about this doctor? She was nice but my doctor prescribed Zoloft, which is an antidepressant medication. So, you can imagine what our first hearing was like when I could not even think straight and there were things I could not remember. My memory of that day was how Mark would make small talk with the magistrate and, I am sure she would think he was charming and a looker, oh how my spirit is struggling to stay alive.

As I waited patiently for my spousal support order to come through and not knowing what the results were going to be, I continued with the therapy and those horrible pills. Then I received that wonderful letter and with the blessing of GOD and this wonderful woman seeing through my husband's charm, I was awarded spousal support and with this wonderful news, I would be able to cover my living expenses. My, how I felt I won the lottery and that no matter what Mark did, they will not take this away from me, that I would be able to pay my bills.

I decided to stop going to therapy and taking those horrible pills. I concentrated on helping my daughter and my granddaughter. When I think about it now, I realize that I stoped taking care of me and was taking care of everyone else. Manuel was arrested and I had no money to bail him out so, he spent some time in prison, why did he get locked up, he tried to steal a car, why did he try to steal a car, god I will never understand and will never know the reason.

Months continued on and I worked on my daughter's bedroom. My future granddaughter was growing inside my daughter and I wanted to paint a positive color for her and the baby's bedroom so I used Lilac. Such a happy and beautiful color, I was so happy doing this for her that, the pain I was feeling inside was kept hidden.

My memory takes me back when Elizabeth was given her first ultra sound and when I found out that it was going to be a little girl, all I could do was cry and all the excitement of my first granddaughter was just wonderful. Elizabeth slept with me through her entire pregnancy. Elizabeth slept with me until the morning her water broke and I took the risk of driving our car and because of my vision we almost crashed into a tree, thank god my daughter saw the tree before I did.

When my granddaughter arrived in this unpredictable world, and the fear of how things were going in this country I watched as she came into the world and I just stared and cried. I was joking around with my daughter and I would say, "Elizabeth this baby is from the milk man. Elizabeth would laugh too." Samantha had reddish blonde hair and her complexion was milky white. I got a closer look at her and she reminded me so much of my deceased brother Arturo.

We brought Samantha and Elizabeth home. Their room was all prepared. What I was not prepared for was that

Elizabeth became very ill right away; Elizabeth was constantly throwing up and was extremely depressed. I did not know what was wrong and I knew that my daughter needed help, so Elizabeth was taken to the hospital and she was admitted into the Hospital and while the doctors were trying to diagnose what was wrong with my daughter, I watched over my granddaughter. This is why the bond between Samantha and I continued until this very day.

Elizabeth was diagnosed with an illness that many women suffer at the birth of their child. I continued to help and protect my daughter and granddaughter and there have been some bumps in the road but my faith in god never went away.

I often thought of my mother in law through all of this, how she portrayed such a holy roller and she was so perfect and so was her son, not realizing the damage these horrible people had left behind. Then I would move on and spent many precious times with my granddaughter.

Manuel called me and begged if I would sign the papers for him to come home on house arrest. My memory of our phone conversation was always, mom I promise, things would be different and I would beg my son to please not to bring home drama. So, I met with a correctional officer and I signed the papers and all I wanted was for my family to be close and to help one another, it did not matter anymore Mark was not a part of our lives we had each other.

The day Manuel arrived home was supposed to be a happy day and it did not turn out the way we all hoped and prayed. Samuel, Mel, his girlfriend at the time, Elizabeth and myself and a old girlfriend of Manuel was there, and all hell broke loose. If my memory serves me right, this young man had all this anger built up inside, and myself and his sister were going to be the blunt of his anger no matter how much we tried to avoid it, he was angry.

Day after day, something would piss him off. Time after time, we tried. Constant phone calls to the police, over and over again and no matter how much I tried to make the peace it just would not stop. One afternoon, I was going through Mark's things and I found a baseball card, I did not give much thought to it so, I gave it to Manuel, well this angered Elizabeth and here we go the fuck again, the fighting got so bad, I had poor Samantha in my arms and Manuel and Elizabeth were fist fighting. Elizabeth grabbed a weapon and ripped up his coat and he hit Elizabeth. The police were called and both Manuel and Elizabeth were taken in because they were both marked up.

I remember one night, another battle took place and it ended with me getting hit and scratched on my neck. If I would tell them to leave, the answer I would get was, "This is daddy's house too." I had it. I could not take another moment of fighting, I had Manuel and Elizabeth removed from my home and as much as it hurt me because of the love I have for them and knowing quite well Elizabeth had a baby I just could not do it anymore. I tried to get Mark to sign the papers to do some small repairs to the house and the idiot refused, he said, "You sign the divorce papers and I will sign the papers for them to do the small repairs on the house so it could be sold". The truth, Mark felt that bitches like me did not deserve anything and he did not want me to have one penny of the house.

I left and I moved to Bensalem, PA. No one knew me there and I was no longer in the Philadelphia area where Mark had a lot of power. I will tell you exactly how much power Mark had. One night I was suppose to have met Yeni at the club and I was not sure, but I thought I saw

Mark and he was not alone. I walked up on him and there he was with Dee and I said, "So this is what you left home for?" Before I knew it, he had the bouncer grab me and I said, "Look, just let me go, I am going and I need to get my purse off the bar." As I walked back to the bar and gathered my belongings, I noticed I still had a full glass of wine and with this, I grabbed the glass of wine walked up on Mark. He turned around and I threw the full glass of wine in his face. Boy was he ever pissed. I walked up to the coat girl and I was about to get my coat. Mark started calling me whore, bitch and all kinds of names and without thinking about it, I smacked him right across the face. This fool continued to call me these horrible names and each time a curse word would come out, I would hit him again.

Not realizing there were several women standing waiting to get into the nightclub when one said, "Hit that motherfucker again!" I finally said, "The great Inspector Stun, you caused me to have retinal detachment and you do not give a damn what you did to me." Mark realized many women were watching him and he walked away.

I was invited to a Mother's Day Banquet and I happen to walk into the ladies room when a friend came up and warned me, This young woman happen to be a corporal on the Philadelphia Police department. Missy said to me, "Watch your back". Mark was going to try everything possible to get me arrested. The overwhelming fear of knowing how much power this man had and what he could do to me finally drove me into hiding.

I moved into my apartment on April 2001 and it was such a modest little place but I was happy. All the drama and not being able to help my children would not consume me any further, so I thought.

I started dating again and realized that there was so much bitter inside of me. I didn't trust men; I felt a man was just good for one thing and one thing only. At times not even the sex was enough to fill the horrible dark hole I couldn't seem to escape.

Jon was someone I met at Michael's nightclub on State Road. When I first got a look at him, I thought, "Wow", this guy has a great body. Jon was a body builder and I must admit he had a great sense of humor. Maybe this is why I continued to date him, I will never know.

Jon and I stopped seeing each other and he tried to explain why he lied to me. The pain from my marriage and the emotional abuse he put his wife through just made me angrier.

One hot afternoon as I was swimming in the pool of the apartment complex and there happen to be several children also in the pool. As I was floating in the 8ft deep part of the pool, I first thought it was the sun and I realize that I had the strangest sensation of needles I could not understand why and then all of the sudden the life guard was screaming from the top of his lung to get out of the pool. Everyone scattered. I swam to the lower end of the pool and grabbed the pole and that's when I felt the electrical shock. No one could explain what exactly took place. Two of the young teenage girls were burnt and the lifeguard had a jolt to his heart. We all looked confused and I decided to go home to my apartment. I realized even after I was taking my shower that I still had the sensation of needles. Around 8 o'clock that evening one of the staff workers called my apartment and asked me if I was alright, I replied, "What's going on?"

I told him that I kept having sensations of needles. He said I should be taken to the hospital right away. My friend Michael Lofton drove me to the hospital.

Everyone who was in the pool was all present at the hospital. We were all trying to figure out what the heck happened and Frank the lifeguard proceeded to fill me in on what took place this afternoon.

Our electric company was running a test and somehow, some way they crossed the wires and the electrical current went to the pool. For years, I would feel constant pins and needles, and test after test were performed. Medication was given to me, but nothing would help the pins and needles. Until this very day, I can be sitting reading or just chatting with someone and I get this jolt of needles.

The attorneys that represented me did a horrible job in handling my case and truthfully, it did not matter. I fired them before my deposition was scheduled and hired my new attorney because they could not find physical proof of my injuries. I am just happy to be alive. I always felt that I had nine lives and that God had me here for a reason. What my calling was I did not know; I know now.

I dated off and on and I met some nice men and not so nice men. I realized I had no trust in men and it consumed me. I continued in that miserable dark hole; did I really love myself? For years I would often wonder, would I ever be able to answer my own questions?
There is a saying, when women have several lover's she is considered a whore, but when man does it, he is a stud. Honestly, I had my share of lovers and this horrible feeling of nothingness was taking over my entire being.

After the pool accident, I continued back and forth to the neurologist; the doctors could not help me. My lease with the apartment complex was coming to an end. Truly, I did not want to leave, but there was so much tension because of the pool accident I felt it was best for me to go. I gave notice to the apartment complex and moved in with my nephew Luis. I thought it would be great; I would be able to save up some money. It did not work out that way. My daughter was living from place to place with my granddaughter and money was so tight for her, I had to help her with expenses,

Many times when I was living at my apartment, I wouldn't have enough to eat because I was sending my daughter money. I felt guilty because I was not there to help her, and Samantha was living in a women's shelter. Things just were not great, Elizabeth was pregnant with my second grandchild and I was not able to help her. My lease was up so I moved in with my nephew. During that time, I realized that things were just horrible. Neither my ex nor Elizabeth's father would extend any help. My ex had the power; he could have helped her with shelter. The other so called father thought he was so great, but he did nothing. Never did he ever offer a shelter for her and her baby. I was in a horrible situation and so was she. I just did not have enough and I thought making her take on responsibility for herself, she could make it. I was wrong.

Not long after the pool accident, my home in Olney was sold as is. I sat next to Mark in the conference room and the entire time I sat there, I felt I never knew this man. Mark had stopped paying the taxes on the home and I never knew this. I trusted him and I believed in him. In the end, my home was worth over $90,000.00 but after everything, from taxes to the other debts I received a total of $700.00. The sadness took over me again; all of my sweat and tears were for nothing. I did most of the painting, striping floors and so much more, and this was my worth, $700.00.?

And it did not matter how much I received I made it a point to divide the money with my children.

I knew at the time of moving out of my apartment was a good decision. Jon's wife continued to pop by every moment she got. I believe it was to see if Jon was at my apartment and as much as I tried to tell her he wasn't, she would continue to stop by anyway. My heart went out to her because I knew the horrible feeling of abandonment.

I continued dating and from time to time, Jon and I would hang out. Everything seemed okay for a bit. Jon and I remained good friends and I made it very clear that I was not about to hurt his wife or ex-wife whichever way he addressed her. I was not going to hurt her.

One afternoon I was extremely bored and was on the computer and I happened to stopped by a black website; it was not Black Planet. I came across a very attractive, tall, nice looking black man. I decided to join the website and I sent him a message. We talked for a bit over the phone and he seemed real nice. I told him a bit about myself and he did the same. He told me he was a Pennsylvania State Trooper and my heart jump very quickly. I promised myself that I would never date another police officer ever again, a state trooper or even a military man. They frightened the hell out of me and this gentleman realized this because I became very silent, I apologized for my silence, I could not help but to be honest with him.

I said, "Damien, no offense to or your profession, but I do not like dating cops." He said, "Carmen, why not?" Then I proceeded to tell him about my marriage and who my husband was and the abuse my children and I went through. I was scared out of my panties and I was about to hang up the phone when Damien said, "Carmen you cannot judge every police officer or state trooper because of what your husband did to you."
I thought he was right. I couldn't judge this man because of what Mark did to me. I proceeded to talk to

him and that following week we decided to meet one another. I took the train to Lancaster, PA and I thought it was such a lovely ride. You could see how beautiful Pennsylvania is. The ride was so nice and once I left Philadelphia I felt a calmness taking over me. I felt happy.

I could not understand why for such a large city it was just so ugly in some areas. I arrived at the train station and there he was, this huge man 6'4, about 300 pounds. I thought to myself, is this real, we just hit it off right away. Damien, said we should first stop at the market, so we could buy several things for the picnic. In my mind I thought, "Wow a picnic, huh?" It was amazing.

We were at the top of the hill and it was breathtaking. We talked and joked around and in all my years of marriage my husband would never take me on a picnic. Mark did not like cooking out and we did not go to the fire works on the 4th of July. We did not take trips until Mami offered to take me to Puerto Rico.

My mother would never admit this to me but she knew Mark was controlling and he did not want me to go to Puerto Rico with her. In the end, my mother gave up her plane tickets and my husband bought three more tickets so the kids could go. This is how we were able to go to Puerto Rico for the first time in my life.

After my visit with Damien, I felt something positive about us and he drove me back to Philadelphia, PA. We promised to get together again real soon.

Jon and I decided to hang out at Tim's Place. This was a small corner bar that belonged to an old friend that was a retired police officer and I always felt safe there. Tim did not care if Mark and I were separated and he welcomed me with open arms. Jon went in and greeted Tim as usual and we went to our usual corner. Because most of my vision came out of my left eye, I made it a point to sit where I could see all of my surroundings. Jon would like to kid around and he notice this one woman he called Elvira. He kept saying, "Look Carmen, look at her." I would say, "Jon, leave that poor woman alone"!

We would laugh and I really did not give it too much thought, it was getting late and the place was getting ready to close. John and I decided to go to a neighborhood Diner. As I was entering the diner, I realized that there were two women behind me. Truthfully, I didn't give it much thought, as we enter the ladies room; I received a phone call from my nephew Luis. I said to Luis, "Hey, I am fine; Jon and I stopped by to have breakfast and afterwards I will be home."

I was joking with one of the young women and I said, "My nephew is worried about me and checking up on me". We both just laughed and as I entered one of stalls and I couldn't help but to overhear one of the young women making comments about me. I thought to myself, "Do I know these women?" As I exited the stall, I couldn't help but ask the young lady if I knew her, but she just gave me a blank stare. I studied her face and I did not know who she was.

I asked her what her name was and I remember so clearly, as though it was yesterday. I continued to study her face and I still did not recognize her. I was so puzzled when she answered with a nickname. I said, "No dear, what is your real name" and with that she responded, "That's right, I am Dee Gonzales." Then it hit me; I was amazed because with my own response, the next word came pouring out of my mouth was. "OH honey, you don't have to worry about me, I don't want him."

You see, this young woman was my husband's mistress; the woman he left his family and our home for. I couldn't believe what came out of her mouth next. Her response to me was, "I know you're only concerned about the pension and alimony." Fuck, it hit me like a ton of bricks, and without thinking I stood tall in front of this woman and I said, "You seem to have forgotten, I am his wife." "Do I bother you?" "Do I bother him?" This irritating little person proceeded to tell me that Mark and her lived together now and she went on and on and on. I asked her, "Why are you bothering me?" I knew about her years before he left. I was so angry and upset. I told this woman she could walk by me a million times and I wouldn't know who she was. Then I asked her, "Do you know about my vision? Do you know what he did to me?" I became angry and approached her closer looking directly into her face. She then told me that Mark was home taking care of their kids. I told her he was a fool, that I always thought he was a fool.

I said to Dee, "You and your girlfriend cornered me in this bathroom and I knew someone was walking behind me and now you're trying to intimidate me." With that, I looked at the both of them and I said, "I will kick you and your girlfriend's ass!!!"

What saved Dee was the waitress that came into the restroom because I was disgusted. I realized this pathetic girl knew who I was but I did not know who she was and that frighten me to no end. I felt my blood pressure rise and Jon was trying to do everything in his power to calm me down. Then, he remembered that they were the two young ladies he was talking about at Tim's place. He remembered them following me into the bathroom. When I arrived at home, I did call the police to make a complaint and they took a report. Lord, I even went downtown to file a personal complaint. Hey, who was I kidding? Mark was Chief Inspector and I was just his emotional soon to be ex-wife who made too much of

Rosaura Torres

this incident. As he told our oldest son Samuel, I was over exaggerating.

III

This overwhelming feeling of fear began to take over and I thought, "I would no longer be safe here in Philadelphia, PA." I knew it was best for me to leave and I remember telling my new friend, the Pennsylvania State Trooper, about what happened. To my surprise, he felt that I should relocate to the Lancaster area.

Damien said, "No one knows you here and you will be safe. I will make sure you get to your doctor's appointment and to the market." I thought, "Wow"! Maybe this would be a good idea for me to relocate and with Damien's help; I began to look for my new apartment.

During the time that I searched for my apartment, Damien and I planned little outings together; we took the Strasburg Train ride, a trip to the Crystal Cave and to the IMAX Theater in Harrisburg, PA.

During one of our afternoons trying to find my new apartment he thought I should schedule an appointment to meet with Erin who was the manager for an apartment complex. I never gave it much thought and the price of the apartment was just a bit over my price range. Later on, I found out this was the same apartment complex that one of his girlfriend's lived in. I remember asking Damien, "Why would you want me to move there?" It just never made any sense to me until much later. Damien was kind enough as to help me locate an apartment; he even helped me fill out the application because of my eyes. I thought, "Wow." What a great guy. Did I truly find someone that really respected me and did not care about my handicap? My vision made me so insecure and very much frightened I thought he would make sure that everything would be safe because that is what he promised me. Foolish me, I believed him.

I finally found a very nice apartment right across the road from Damien. It was large and perfect for me. One afternoon I had to travel to my new apartment; I took the train and I met with a representative from Sterling Place and I signed the papers. It was getting late and I knew I had to head back to Philadelphia. I tried to call Damien to see if he would be kind enough as to drop me off at the train station. I thought it was not such a big deal and I stopped by his place; as I said before, Damien lived right across the road. I waited for a few minutes and then he pulled up, and we both walked into his home but I could tell he was angry and then he began to yell and scream at me and I was speechless. I could not believe my ears with this horrible treatment; so, I quietly called a cab and left without a word.

Through my entire train ride back home, I could not understand why this man would change and speak so cruel to me. I then started blaming myself for the way he was treating me. Maybe he was tired or maybe something happened at work. I could not explain his behavior.

When I arrived at my nephew's home I did not even bother to call him, I went on with my regular routine. The following morning after coffee, I went to check my email and this is what was waiting for me in my inbox. The email was dated on August 23, 2002 at 8:33 am. The subject of the email was, "I'm truly sorry☹." "The email went like this"!

"Carmen,

I know you probably don't care to hear from me right now but there are some things I need to say. You've been nothing but nice to me and I have an explanation for my actions. I can't justify my actions but I can explain it. You see it has nothing to do with you or taking you to the train station itself. The problem is this…When I get off from work, it drives me crazy when I have zero time for myself before I have to go to bed and right back to work. I knew that between going shopping, taking you to the train station, fixing dinner and fixing lunch for the next day, I wouldn't have any time at all before having to go to bed. I can't take that. To me it's almost like working 24 hrs. Straight, I have to have some time in between shifts to just relax and unwind. When I don't get that, it makes me miserable. I know probably now think I have the evil side of myself that you haven't seen until now. I don't. I'm the same person you've always known. I don't know why I got that angry. I guess I was just feeling really drained. I know it doesn't help now, but after I calmed down, I did come outside to get you and take you to the train station. But you were gone. I didn't even hear the cab come. So if you rather never hear from me again, I'll understand. I'd kind of expect that. However, I do miss talking to you. I miss everything about our friendship. You are a good woman. Even in a fit of anger, I can see that.

Now that I got that off my chest, how are you doing? I hope you got everything straightened out with the apartment. I'm at work right now, haven't been feeling too good. I went home early Wednesday, and took off sick Thursday. My hip started killing me. I could barely get out of bed. I stopped taking the pain medication I was on a few months ago. It was causing bleeding in my stomach. When I stopped taking it, I didn't have any more pain. I think it just took this much time for the effects of the prescription for me. I started taking medicine again. I got some relief from the pain, but it takes several days before it gets into my system completely.

I'm going down to pick up Yan after work. Our weekends together are kind of screwed up because of her camps and visiting her grandmother in Virginia. I'll be around this weekend if you find it in your heart to forgive me. If not, I'll understand.

Damien,
Still Papi"

When I received this email, always giving men the benefit of the doubt, I thought maybe he was having a horrible day and I forgave him for showing me an evil side. I thought, "Maybe things will be better".

One of my weekends visiting Damien, he became ill and had a temperature of 104 and we ended up at Lancaster Memorial Regional Hospital. I felt so sorry for Damien; it turned out his father had a history of prostate cancer. Damien was constantly being tested for it too and I thought it was an excellent ideal. When I think of it now, Damien was a bit paranoid and had every right to be, especially when his father was very ill. It turned out Damien was very constipated and the doctor prescribed a laxative. Now, I am sure you're wondering why I am writing all of this. I remember how I showed nothing but kindness towards him and how cruel he became towards me.

Knowing how ill he became, I became worried about him. One afternoon I could not reach him and when I tried to call, I then received this horrible email from Damien. It went like this:

Rosaura Torres

8/28/2002 8:44:12 EDT
SUBJECT: What's wrong with you?

Well....you managed to do it again. Didn't I say I was going to call you tonight do you think, that I just tell you that? I've been trying to fill out these medical forms for surgery all evening, but I can't even concentrate on what I'm supposed to be doing because the God damned phone keeps ringing every ten minutes. Why do you do if I tell you I'm going to call, and then I'm going to call? I have caller I.D. for God's sake. You don't have to call me 18 f_king times for me to know you called. I'm so pissed right now I don't even want to talk to you.

Damien
"Wow"! I could not believe this man was acting like this again. Damien acted like such an infant when we were in the hospital and when you show a man like him any kind of kindness they start to show you their horrible verbal abusive side. The signs were all there, and they it showed loud and clear. God forgive me for ignoring the signs.

Then he apologized repeatedly and foolish me, I forgave him for his verbal abuse. I remember one afternoon I had moved his blinds over and he freaked out. Damien started yelling that he paid $100.00 dollars for those blinds; "It's not easy to replace them, "he yelled. I could not understand how one minute this man was kind and the next minute he continued to show an evil side. He then would apologize again and I would forgive him.

My next trip to be to complete the paper work and to get my keys, my son's ex-fiancée Lucy and I drove to out to Sterling Place Apartment to finish up all the work. This particular afternoon, Lucy and I got lost. Lucy was not familiar with the area and I could barely make out the high way signs so we were lost for four hours.

157

When we arrived, I finished all my paper work and asked for directions back to Philadelphia. The management was not able to help us so I said to Lucy, "We can stop at Damien's home and he will be able to help us." Damien was pissed when he saw me; he even accused me of bringing another man to his home. This idiot thought my son's fiancée Lucy was a man. You see, he was still seeing his old girlfriend, Reese.

Damien once described her and he made her sound so sad and pathetic. I listened to how Reese had relocated to the area from California.

I saw all the warning signs and things were so obvious what he thought of women. Damien had promised marriage to Reese and he had no intention to marry her. Then he spoke of Denise; "She is a sick bitch", he said. Damien said her ex-husband and his brothers raped her and she had some mental issues because of it. I couldn't believe my ears. This man spoke of these women as though they were nothing. When I sat and listened as he spoke of them, I realized how much I had confided in him about the abuse that I sustained from my husband. I wondered to myself if he would talk about me in the same rotten way he had spoken of these other women. I felt sorry for Reese because of what Damien told me.

How wrong I was. Reese saw me and she didn't look very happy. Then Damien accused me of kicking his door; that was a lie. He got caught and the only way men like Damien handle a situation like this is to blame the other person.

If Damien thought I was such a horrible person, why would he take the time to print out directions for me? I've never threatened, cursed or even screamed at this man.

After he handed me the directions, I left. I had no intention of staying there any longer.

I received another one of Damien sweet, kind, loving emails and it went like this:

8/30/02
6:37:02 EDT
No subject.

"Before today, I thought you were just emotional, but now I know you truly "psycho". And to think, you came to my unannounced once again with the lame excuse that you needed directions. Do you think I'm stupid? You came for one reason and one reason only and that is to see Reese and to make a scene. I told you, Suzanne was taking me to the hospital, and you just couldn't accept it. Now I know why guys tell lies to women....because when we tell the truth you can't handle it. So you get some guy to drive you all the way up here just to make a complete fool of yourself. Well guess what. It worked. You did a thorough job of embarrassing yourself. I'm beginning to think Stun was right. You're acting just like a North Philly Hood Rate. You know...if there was any chance of us having any kind of relationship, you ruined it I don't want you to have any excuses to try to contact me. I will deliver it to the Sterling Place office. I don't want to see your face again EVER. Please do me a favor. Lose my number! Don't send me any text messages! Lose my email address....and just forget you ever met me! Don't waste time emailing me either. I won't get them. Your email address has already been permanently blocked. Oh yes....and if you ever come to my house again for anything (especially kicking my front door like that), there were be an arrest warrant for Disorderly Conduct, Harassment (and anything else I can think of) waiting for you when you try to move to Sterling Place. IF YOU THINK I'M JOKING TRY ME!!!

Damien"

Good Lord, I could not believe this email. I never kicked his door and I knew very well about Reese. Reese did not know about me. Damien's temper was outright ugly and no matter what I said or did, this man showed an abusive side.

So many nights that I spent with him and even the night we spent at the hospital, he showed me kindness by serving me breakfast in bed for staying up with him. Damien also had a sleeping disorder. Many times, I would shake him awake because he would stop breathing and that frightened me so much.

Many times, I could not sleep and I would go to the back porch and sit, or I would sleep on the sofa. Because of his snoring, I would stay close by because I thought he would stop breathing. I stopped going to the back porch because the neighborhood skunk scared the heck out of me and I was not going to take another risk like that again.

One weekend when I came to visit, he asked me to please take a cab and he would meet me at his home. He asked me to please wait in the back of the house. He said did not care too much for several of his neighbors, especially the one directly across the street. Was I missing something, or could it be that I was ignoring a message that God was trying to tell me?

I was so offended when he called me a North Philly Hood Rat and I felt I deserved an apology. I never called this man out of character and didn't understand why he felt the need to call me out of character. My God, he even mentioned my husband and I thought to myself, did he speak to Mark? Were they trying to hurt me? So many thoughts went through my mind and as much as I tried to analyze the horrible treatment, I could not come up with an answer.

The fact that he would threaten to have me arrested truly left me speechless. Why would this man try to bring up false charges against me? How incredible and erratic his behavior was becoming. Again, Damien apologized for calling me a North Philly Hood Rat and for threatening to bring up false charges against me. Of course, I again accepted his apology.

My relationship with Damien was kind of strained and we were still physical. Damien was a freak! He enjoyed having anal sex; this is the only kind of sex he wanted to have. Wow, he even showed me certain types pornography on his State Police Laptop. I thought to myself, "He is a State Trooper and the law. What do I know? I felt in my gut something was just not right, but I ignored it. I always wondered if he was on the Down Low?

Jon came to visit me and it was great seeing him. I notice he was not feeling well and we just sat in my apartment and watched movies. I was happy to see my old friend. A week after his visit, he felt I should get tested for the Aids Virus and I asked, "Why?" He was also being tested. As it turned out, this breaks my heart to say this; Jon was diagnosed with bone cancer.

I also had to inform Damien that it was best that he also get tested. Before I found out Jon results, Damien turned into a pile of nothing and was an emotional basket case. Then I received this email from Damien: 9/23/2002 Mon PM 12:39:27 EDT

Carmen,

I just got an email from Reese. Her Cancer has gotten worse and she doesn't have the money or insurance to get treatment. She can only get free medical treatment if she is completely poor. Because she works part time for herself and she doesn't qualify for medical aid. I don't know why all of this is happening to us. We are all good people who never hurt anybody. I can't stop thinking about this. I feel like my whole life has been turned upside down. I started to leave work early, but that would not help. All I would do is worry all day and night. You are a kind, giving person. I've decided that whatever the outcome is with my situation and yours, I'm going to stick by you. I'm going to be there for you even if you end up negative. I just wanted you to know that.

Damien

My results turned out negative and after receiving this email from Damien, I thought maybe things would be better, or so I hoped.

Then, as quickly as things seemed to be going well, something evil and horrible happened. Damien's emotional rollercoaster was just too much for me. He did nothing but lie and I allowed this man to treat me like dirt and verbally abuse me. I continued to forgive him for the abuse.

Damien abuse started all over again and I could not take it anymore. I wanted to show him how erratic and abusive his behavior had become. This one afternoon after work, I went by to see him. We were on the phone talking and I kept saying to him, "Let me show you why I want to speak to you". This is when I realized he was not coming to his place anytime soon. So, I left. I set my alarm for 6:30 the following morning September 27, 2002. I wanted to show Damien how disturbed he had become. When I got to his block, I notice his car was parked on the street and I waited for him to come out.

Rosaura Torres

There was no yelling, screaming, or arguing. I watched as Damien came out of his house and in a whisper, I said to him, "Damien can we speak later on this evening so I can show you what I have been trying to show you?" Damien said, "OKAY." It was normal for me to be in the State Police car; I had been picked up from the train station and the super market before, so when I asked if he could please give me a ride across the road, I didn't give it much thought. I couldn't remember if he said yes or no, maybe he said no. I noticed he was moving things from the passenger side of the seat and I started walking around in front of the car. As I approached the passenger side of the car and grabbed the door, he hit the gas and I jerked and went forward. I was afraid of falling so I held on to the side view mirror and I thought he was going to stop. He didn't stop; he kept going with me on the side of the State Police car.

I was holding on until he hit the brakes and that is when I went flying and hit the concrete. I lost consciousness for about a minute or so and I struggled to get myself off the ground, I don't know how it was possible for me to stand and get on my feet. I noticed everything was so fuzzy and blurry. I started to walk toward the main road and I noticed Damien had made a u-turn. I touched my head and realized I was bleeding. As I slowly walked toward the main road, Damien pulled up and asked me if I was all right and I said, "NO". I am hurt and I need help. I asked Damien if he could get me back to my apartment and he said "NO". Then I asked him if he could get me to the hospital and he said no again and drove away.

I could not believe what just happened. I was alone, bleeding trying to walk and trying to make sense of what just happened to me. I wondered how this man of the law could leave me here alone!!! Coward, nothing but a low down dirty dog!!!
Damien left me in the middle of the road as if I was an animal. I could not believe he left me there and I kept

163

praying to GOD to help me please, get me home alive and safe. Damien would call my cell phone and I said, "You have to come back." He said he was running late for work and he hung up the phone. I felt as though everything was going in slow motion and all I could do was pray.

I tried to climb up the little side hill where my apartment was located at but I slid down and I had to walk all the way around to get to my apartment. Damien and I were on the phone again and I begged him to please come back and get me to the hospital. He told me to ask one of my neighbors. He was fully aware that he was the only person I knew in Lancaster, PA.

I had just relocated to Lancaster, PA from Philadelphia, PA. Then told me to call the police and I asked him, "What do you want me to tell the police, Damien?" He wanted me to lie. He wanted me to tell them that I fell and I said to him, "You want me to lie for you, just like I did for Mark." Then he hung up the phone. When I finally got into my apartment and saw what he had done to me, I called him and left a message on his answering machine. I said I am going to give you the benefit of the doubt, that you will come back and take me to the hospital. I realized I could not wait, I was feeling very sick to my stomach and I felt like I was going to vomit. I called the police and I told them what happened, and how he left me there in the middle of the road bleeding and begging for help.

Officer Richard entered the ambulance and all I could do was cry. I kept telling him, I want to believe in my heart he did not mean to hurt me, but he wanted me to lie to the Police.

I was taken to Regional Memorial Hospital in Lancaster, PA,

and I could not even see straight. I knew something was wrong with my vision but I prayed it was not what it turned out to be. As I was being examined, a Lt. Moore from the Lancaster Police Department came into my room and he told Officer Richard that he did not see anything wrong with me. As politely, as Officer Richard could, he motioned the

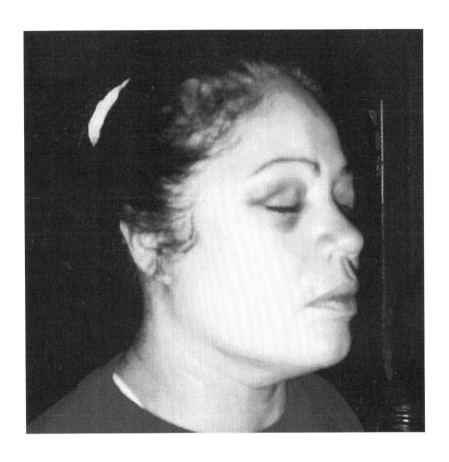

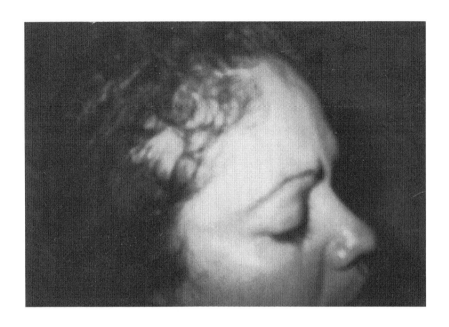

Rosaura Torres

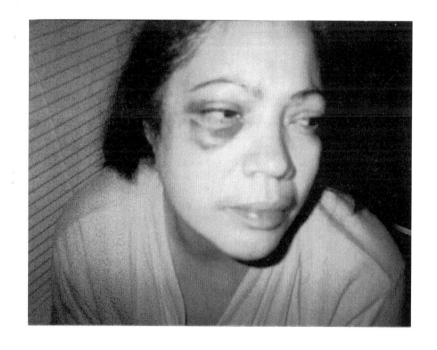

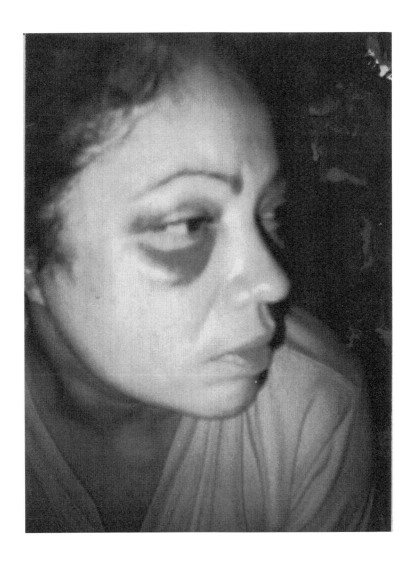

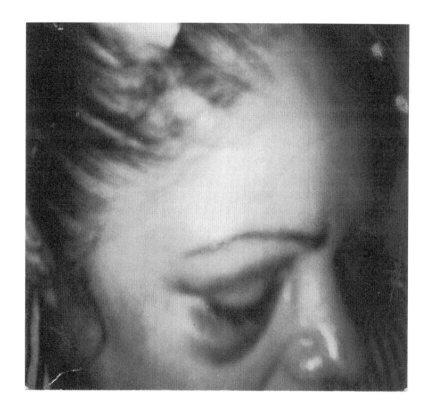

Lt. to the side of my bed; this is when he saw the results of my injuries.

I repeated everything I said to the Lt. Moore just as I told it to Officer Richard; "I want to believe in my heart that Damien did not mean to hurt me but he wanted me to lie to the Police.

Lt. Moore waited while the doctor ran several more tests on me. I was released from the hospital with a severe head concussion and abrasions to my arm, leg and head. I was first driven to where the assault took place and then I was taken to the Detective Bureau where Lt. Moore interviewed me. There are things I just do not remember about the interview. My girlfriend Wanda called me and I told her what happened; she told me to call my lawyer. I do remember Lt. Moore saying that Damien made a foolish, foolish mistake but I don't remember much else.

The Lt. dropped me off and my sons arrived to see the condition I was in. Manuel really wanted to hurt Damien, but I told him we must let the law take care of this. As I spoke to my sons, my son Manuel was taking pictures of my injuries. I still could not believe what happened to me and how Damien left me there in the middle of the road begging for help.

After the accident, I was back and forth to the doctor's office. My head concussion caused me so much pain for months after the assault. What really hurt me the most was that the jelly from the left eye had detached and it was only a matter of time before I would need surgery. The doctors at Wills Eye Hospital continued to monitor my vision. I waited for two weeks for Internal Affairs to come and interview me about the horrible abuse. It was never recommended by the Lt. to get a protection order of abuse. I found out later on that it is the procedure of many police departments' throughout all our great states. I followed my own instincts and called Women against Abuse in the area. I met with one of the supporters from the organization and she recommended that I retain an attorney who would help me get my protection order.

The law firm that was recommended to me was Madmen Legal Service, and the attorney that represented me was Lucy L. Beanman.

I was granted a temporary (order of protection) on October 7, 2002. I wish I could give you the date when I met Corporal Duffy and Corporal Richard. I do know it took place two weeks after the horrible abuse from Damien. When the Troopers arrived and I shook both their hands, Corporal Duffy commented about how my face was still bruised from the injuries.

Corporal Richard had a particular look on his face. From my experiences with my husband, I remember the look. It's a look you get when someone is trying to see if they can catch you in a lie. Funny, I gave the trooper the same look and he did not intimidate me.

Before my interview was taken, Corporal Duffy repeated himself on three separated occasions. He said, "I find it hard to believe Damien would leave you in the middle of the road because I have known Damien for 15 years." He first, made this comment before the recording. Then after the recording and then made the same statement again when we drove to where the assault took place.

I finally realized these men were not there to help me. They were going to do everything in their power to protect Trooper Sober and I was in a world of trouble. No matter what they said, or how they tried to make me feel uncomfortable, I was not going to go away quietly and I promised myself that I would continue forward.

When the horrible abuse took place, my son Samuel called his father. Samuel told his father what had happened and explained how the trooper would not help or call an ambulance. In the police procedures and policies, they have guidelines. As a Chief Inspector Mark felt that as a law enforcement officer that even if Damien did not want to physically take me to the hospital, it was still his duty to call an ambulance and render me aid. That is the LAW.

When I gave my testimony to Corporal Duffy, I told him exactly what I told Lt. Moore; "I told that I wanted to believe in my heart he did not mean to hurt me, but he wanted me to lie to the Police". Even after I gave my testimony to the corporal, I received a threatening phone call from someone telling me to drop the charges or else. I wonder if I would be protected.

A week or so later, I received a phone call from Corporal Duffy. He wanted to know if I wanted to add or change anything in my story and I said, "No", everything I said to you was the honest truth." His response to me was, "They are going to give Trooper Sober the option of adding or changing anything in his story." I said, "You can give Damien anything you want". My whole entire being was shaking because of the way these men used their power.

I received a letter from the court telling me I have my hearing for my order of protection. The hearing was rescheduled on November 4, 2002. To my surprise, Corporal Duffy was also there and I did not understand why? In my gut I knew this man was not there for me, but why was he there? On November 4, 2002, my order of protection was taken away from me. I broke down because I had pictures, and emails as proof but still the District Attorney withdrew my order. They said it was because of the statement I made saying, "I want to believe in my heart Damien did not want to hurt me, but he wanted me to lie."

Sweet Lord, I could not believe it; I sat there crying and I could see the look on my attorney's face. What just happen was wrong; there was nothing else she could do.

On December 27, 2002, I received a letter from Attorney Beanman, and the letter went like this:

Dear Ms. Stun:
You should have received a copy of the Defiant Trespass Letter that I sent to Mr. Sober in November. I mailed the letter by both regular mail and certified, restricted delivery to put him on notice.

I recently received the certified mail back as unclaimed. However, the regular mail was never returned and I also sent a copy to Mr. Sobers' attorney. I just wanted to inform you of the above in case you would need that information to show that Mr. Sober was on notice not to contact you or come to your home.

I hope you are doing well, best wish for a safe and happy new year.

Very truly yours,

LEGAL SERVICES

L L. B., Esquire

What do you think the first thought was that came to my head, "What the fuck is this?" This is just horrible! They took my protection order from abuse away from me and then she put him on notice. This made no sense. Was the attorney protecting herself because she knew I was denied protection from a State Trooper? Damien was being protected by those who were supposed to protect me, the victim. Instead, the law ignored the horrible abuse and neglect.

I received nothing from the courts; no matter what, I believed there was a higher power than us all. Eventually, I would receive my justice.

I tried to get out of my obligation to my lease at the apartment complex. Unfortunately, they wanted a sum of money I did not have. I was overcome by fear but I wanted to be brave and to show everyone how strong I was.

The abrasions on my head caused me to lose a lot of my hair. I stayed with Daisy a couple of times when I had a doctor's appointment. It would be just for overnight. I didn't care for her live-in boyfriend and he did not care for me. Whom are we kidding; this man was a bum and he did nothing for her except to add to her expenses.

The week of Thanksgiving, my daughter Elizabeth was preparing for the birth of her son Jacob. Yes, I had a new grandson and she needed my help. I stood by my daughter's side as she tried to give natural birth. Sadly, she was unable to. Elizabeth was given a cesarean section as I watched the doctors cut my daughter open and all I could say in Spanish was, "Oh God, look what they are doing to my baby." Then I saw this huge, beautiful, baby boy and I held my grandson for the first time. I didn't want to let go.

I stayed with Elizabeth for about a week to help her with the children and I knew it was time to go back to my apartment. So, I returned to my apartment and left my family back in New Jersey.

I spent that Christmas alone and afraid. The snowstorm of December 2002 was horrible. My wonderful neighbor Ted tried to check up on me but I was so afraid I would not open the door to him. I had the flu at this time, so I just slept and hid under the blankets.

My suspicions began to grow when my support checks went missing twice. Maybe once would have been okay, but twice and I had no money for food. My Christmas dinner was grits and white rice and even then, I felt blessed. I was alone and afraid and no matter what, I knew God was there right with me. I was ashamed to tell my parents what had happened to me. I called my girlfriend Maria and she was so upset about how I was treated. I thank God for her love and support because no matter what anyone tried to say, I did not deserve this horrible abuse. My friend Maria was a retired Philadelphia Police Officer. Throughout the years, she and her sister Margie have always kept me in their prayers. I know now more than ever that God did hear their prayers.

My mother became very ill with dementia and most people with dementia do not remember a lot, but not Mami. She was aware of everything; but at times mother did forget how to swallow and to walk. For two years, my sweet, strong, wonderful mother laid in a bed and slowly we watched as the strength of our family slowly withered away.

On February 9, 2003, I was finally completely exhausted and frustrated. I needed to know what the outcome of the investigation from internal affairs was, so I placed the phone call. I spoke with Corporal Duffy and he said, "It was up to Damien's commander to make the decision about what will happen." I was then transferred to Major

Pew. During the time of my abuse, the Major was a Captain. He had just been promoted to Major. I congratulated this man on his promotion and then I got right down to the point, I wanted to know the outcome of the investigation.

The Major proceeded to tell me that it would be my word against Damien's and the Police believed he did nothing wrong in not rendering me any aid. Therefore Damien would not be charged or disciplined for the abuse I suffered by him. I couldn't believe my ears. As calmly as I could, I asked him if he could please send me the report in writing. He wanted to know why I wanted it in writing, and I said, "Because my attorney needs it". He also wanted to know who my attorney was; at that time, it was Pete Bauer. I thanked him for all his help and at no time did I yell, scream or cry on the phone. I calmly hung up the phone and sank down onto the floor and just cried and cried. Somehow I knew when the investigation was first taking place that the law that was supposed to protect me was not going uphold their sworn duty to me as a citizen. They had always protected each other; I now knew that this would be no different.

I gathered myself together, I sat in front of my computer, and I started to write a letter to our new Governor Russell. I proceeded to write and tell him what had happen to me and how I was left in the middle of the road bleeding and begging for help. I also made it quite clear that I believed there was a cover-up within the state police. Sadly and with disappointment, I never heard from my governor or from anyone in his office.

I tried for days after that to keep a positive attitude about life and then it happened. On February 17, 2003, I was rushed to Will's Eye Hospital and during my examination, the retina in the left eye had detached in three separate places. I was scheduled for surgery the

Rosaura Torres

following morning. I felt a horrible dark shadow taking over my spirit and the loneliness of the past coming back to haunt me.

There was a severe snowstorm and my future daughter-in-law Lucy drove from Monmouth County to Lancaster, PA to pick me up and drive me to Philadelphia, PA to Will's Eye Hospital. I did not know how I could ever repay this wonderful woman for the love and compassion she showed me. She helped me during the worse time of my life.

I remember the operating room nurse asking me where my family was. I sadly said, "I am alone", and then I started to cry. I went into surgery thinking I was going to die; I even told the doctor to make sure I wake up please. I gave one doctor a difficult time; he wanted to numb the area of the eye and I said, "NO WAY, YOU WILL PUT ME COMPLETELY TO SLEEP!" We went back and forth until he realized I was not going to allow them to perform any surgery on me until they put me completely to sleep.

I awoke from my surgery and I felt horrible. I became quite ill, my blood pressure was up, and then I began to vomit. The same night I called Daisy and told her that I just had surgery on my left eye. Daisy's sister was an attorney and I needed her legal advice. She believed I should not press charges or sue this trooper because I would embarrass my husband. I could not believe my ears and I could care less about embarrassing anyone. This abuse happened, period. I knew right then I had to remove myself for a while. The next morning I was released from the hospital and Jon was kind enough to pick me up from the hospital and drop me off at my parents' home. In a million years, I could not thank Jon enough for the kindness he showed me when I was severely injured.

The entire week I was at my parents' home and the state of turmoil I was in was just outright horrible. I couldn't eat and all I wanted to do was sleep. My sweet, wonderful father tried to get me to eat. At night Papi, would bring me Chamomile tea, which I would happily drink. Food was the last thing on my mind.

I had my best vision in my left eye and now I didn't even have that. I was so depressed and bitter because I didn't know what the outcome of my surgery would be and how much of my vision would return. My girl Sonia, who was one of my old friends from Camden, New Jersey, was kind enough to drive me back to Wills Eye Hospital for my next check-up before I went back to my apartment. By then, I was deeply depressed.

"Please God," I prayed, "Be merciful and give me something back, just a little something, anything, and I will be grateful." I returned to Lancaster, PA a week after my surgery. I didn't want to stay in Jersey and bring any more strain to my father. My mother was very ill and my brother Ralph was sick as well. He was diagnosed with Hepatitis C and was still on Methadone treatment, because of his prior drug addiction to heroin. This so-called medication was doing more harm than good to my brother. I knew that I had to leave because I did not want my mother to see me like this. She would often say to me "Why didn't you tell me?" I would say, "Mami, I am so sorry, I was ashamed of myself." My son Samuel and Lucy came to pick me up and drove me back to Lancaster, PA. They stayed for a bit, but not long. I knew I would have to place the drops in my eyes and take care of myself. I was blessed to have my wonderful neighbor Ted in my life at this time. Ted took me to the market and to the drug store; he watched over me. One of the assistants from the apartment complex was kind enough to pick up my mail and bring it to me. It was still very cold and the snow made the sidewalk and roads icy. I was afraid to walk up the hill to pick up my mail.

I would not travel alone and I stayed very close to home. My daughter had to leave her apartment and I asked Daisy if she would be willing to help her out for just a bit until I returned. Her boyfriend didn't want any part of my daughter and Daisy didn't want to make waves with him. Elizabeth came out to Lancaster with the children. I never told her, but I was happy to see her and the kids. I rented a bed for my daughter; I slept with Samantha and Elizabeth slept with Jacob. My little guy was only five months old.

As the months continued on, I knew that it would be for the best that we relocate back to Philadelphia. My daughter Elizabeth could be quite bossy and from day one, that's exactly how she was. There were constant arguments and so much bitterness from her and I just didn't know why. I thought that because she knew of the horrible experience that I went through, she would be more compassionate but I was wrong. Then, my son Manuel came to live with us.

My brother Ralph called me and said that it was only a matter of time before Mami would not be with us. Though I knew it was coming, I just didn't want to believe it. I knew that I was so much like my mother and I decided to return to their home to clean and prepare my mother's room. I even scrubbed the kitchen cabinets. The bathroom needed a very good cleaning. My mother's bed was now sitting in the middle of our living room and I would talk to her daily.

Mami knew everything that was going on but I would hear her call out to her mother and father. She would say, "I am not ready to go. They still need me." I couldn't believe my ears. Even on her deathbed, my mother worried about her babies, though we were no longer

babies. We were all adults, and she was still afraid that we were not going to be able to survive without her.
I returned to my apartment and a week later on July 3, 2003, my mother Isabella De La Rosa Ortiz went home to be with her love ones.

My mother was the youngest of 11 children and Mami was the last of her brothers and sisters to go home. I knew my mother was preparing for her journey home but I couldn't accept the fact that she was now gone forever.

I prepared my Mami's home, as she would want it. I cleaned and had her hospital bed removed so my father would not be upset. My siblings and I were preparing for the funeral and while going through Mami's financial matters we discovered that there was not enough money to bury her. Family is supposed to come together in a time of need, but not my family. There was always anger and fighting and I couldn't understand why. If they weren't arguing about money, it was about something else. My friend Sonia's mother died a month before my mother and we were both taking their deaths very hard. I could feel my mother's presence all around me and Sonia felt the same way. We were like two little kids hurting from the loss of our mothers.

My brother's girlfriend Jenny found it in her heart to pay for my mother's funeral arrangements and to pay for her burial plot. She paid for my father's as well. No matter what the occasion, this dysfunctional family of mine would always break out into a fight. God help us all.

Between Elizabeth, Luis my nephew and my father and I, we put our money together. It was not much but we were able to buy cold cuts, chips and sodas to feed our guests. It is truly amazing that with just a little, we were able to do so much; God is good.

My mother was buried and her love and strength remain with me always. No matter what, I could still always hear my mother say to me, "Carmen, continue the fight because you deserve better than that". So with those wonderful words, I continued forward.
Isabella De La Rosa Ortiz July 13, 1921 – July 3, 2003

"Keep her in your minds and in your hearts. That's the way she would like to be remembered, not with a whole lot of sadness but rather with love and humor. Mom always had a smile or a comical remark about life, even in the face of adversity and suffering. Even at the end when she knew she did not have long to live I believe that her relatives and children that passed before her came to beckon her on, calling to her, "Isabella, es el tiempo." She said "No, not yet," as it was her nature always to be more concerned about others. Although, she wanted to go right then, she waited just a little bit longer for us to accept God's plan for her and for all of us.

So do not be sad or afraid. All her suffering in this world is finished. We may honor her departure best by continuing to love and respect one another and look to help one another with grace and humor, as she did. Let her spirit soar to the Heaven. She taught us a lot about life and the meaning of giving and sharing with others.

Good-bye, Mom; we will miss you but remember, you will always be in our hearts.

Peace, Love you always."

Written by my brother, Lee, Jr.

My husband showed compassion and paid his last respects to my mother. I was not able to shake my husband's hand. It was just five months ago that I had my second retinal detachment surgery because of the abuse. He was the beginning and the trooper was the end of my vision. I was a better person now; I thanked him for coming although I could not find it in my heart to go near him.

The anger from the past abuse showed its ugly head and I continued to ride on a merry-go-round that would last for years. My trust issue had taken over every part of me and I just didn't know what to do. Elizabeth, Manuel, the children and I moved back to Philadelphia, PA area only a month after my mother was buried. It was not a very nice apartment. It was a dump and the carpet was dirty. The stove had so much grease that I had to use a butter knife to scrape it off. I remember being on my hands and knees scrubbing the kitchen and bathroom floors. You may be wondering why my daughter Elizabeth was not helping me. Well, she was never one to clean and I often used to think she loved watching me clean. I always felt that not only my husband, but my children also love to watch me clean. Many times, I couldn't understand why I continued to allow anyone to treat me like this, but that's exactly what I did.

In May of 2003, there was a huge investigation that revealed the unbelievable abuse of power within the state police and how they covered up so many abuses from rape, sexual abuse, harassment and domestic violence. Maybe Governor Russell did read my letter. but I will never know. Many heads were spinning.

The constant fighting with my children was making me sick. Manuel and Elizabeth would use me like a ping pong ball and no matter how much I would try to make the peace, I just couldn't stop their constant bickering. Manuel was so angry because I would tell him to go out and get a job. This strong, handsome son of mine would say, "You never made Samuel or Elizabeth look for work." I tried to help them all, time and time again.

I started dating Mario. Initially, Mario said his family would not accept me. There were comments made to him about dating someone from his own race.

My first Thanksgiving Dinner with his family will always be with me and "here we go again." We drove up to Connecticut where I met his sisters, mother and father. I never hid who I was or who my ex-husband was. It was nothing to be proud of though. Not realizing what a hypocrite Mario's sister was, I thought I was just having a sincere conversation with her. I told her about the abuse that took place in my marriage and about how much my son Manuel loved his father. Elizabeth and Samuel did love their father but Manuel always had a certain bond with Mark. Well, it turned out that "Ms. Thing" wanted to know about my children and me. She must have talked to some of the same people my ex mother-in- law knew and she called my son Manuel a ticking time bomb. The only person I knew who would speak of my children negatively in this manner would be Mark or Doris. I was highly upset. Aida portrayed herself to be a religious person and the memory of my ex mother-in-law and the pain came flooding back all over again.

I was now dating a man who, at times only thought of himself as my therapist, because for years my children who used me for years as their emotional punching bag. Samuel was living in New Jersey so he did not bring me any drama. Sadly, Manuel and Elizabeth were a different story. I tried to keep us together as a family. Our neighbor's upstairs were the "neighbors from hell." The young woman would blast music late at night and I would have to call the police. No matter what I did, this continued repeatedly.

One night, all hell broke loose as my neighbors' brother and father broke down my door. My neighbors' evil daughter used mace on Elizabeth my granddaughter and me. For over a year, I was back and forth in court. Finally, the young woman was charged with assault. The uncle was not charged, because we did not see him, but we heard his voice. They moved out because there was an order of protection against them. I felt for the first time that the legal system had not failed me.

Finally, after so many years, Mark and I were in the legal process of getting our divorce. What Mark never knew, but I remembered was how his girlfriend approached me two years earlier and informed me that she and Mark were living together. The smartest thing I did was to inform my attorney of all this information. A month before our divorce was final, the magistrate wanted information about our finances, and of course, I had none. I had filed all the legal documents my attorney requested and the following month we were set to go to court.

The day before court I was carrying my grandson in my arms when I was walking and I didn't see the hole which was right in front of me, and in I went. In order to protect Jacob I twisted and I injured my knee. I was taken to the hospital and my leg looked like a big balloon; I needed three stitches. Oh, how I felt like a cat. How many more lives did I have left and when would I realize that my vision would never be the same? I had to be extremely cautious where I stepped and walked.

When I entered the courtroom, my soon to be ex-husband had this look on his face like, "Now what happened to her?" My lawyer could not believe my luck. We waited as the lawyers' first spoke and then we were asked to enter the court room. As the magistrate of the court was going over his paper work he asked me, what happened to me and I told him exactly what happened.

The magistrate of the court asked me questions such as who I lived with, etc. I told him who I lived with, which was my daughter and grandchildren. Then it was Mark's turn. He gave them his address. The magistrate asked who he lived with and he said, "Alone." Bingo! I leaned over to my attorney and I said, "Cross examine him." That's when Peter said, "Mr. Stun isn't it true that you live with a Dee Gonzales?" With that, Mark looked flustered and stuttered his words. He finally said "YES." When Mark responded to his answer, not only I, but everyone else turned and looked at him. Everyone in the court saw him for what he was...a liar. One of Elizabeth's friends came to court with me and she said, "When your husband came out of the court room he was pissed and kept saying fuck, fuck, fuck." Many people would not believe this, but I believe GOD was sitting there holding my hand and watching over me.

Two or three weeks later, we were back in court. This was the day my divorce was finalized. As I sat waiting to be seen by the magistrate, my attorney and Mark's attorney were talking and trying to come up with a settlement. My lawyer approached me and said that Mark wanted to give me give an insurance policy in my name for the amount $250,000.00 if he should die, and I did not touch his pension money. With this comment, I looked at my attorney and I said, "NO," this motherfucker might live forever. I want what the court grants me." This was the end of that chapter in my life.

We all sat and listened very closely to what the magistrate had to say. The magistrate granted me my alimony and he informed me that I would also get a part of the DROP Program Fund when Mark retires. I was also granted a part of his pension money for the rest of my life and when he said this all I could think was, "Hey Mark, remember what you said, "bitches like me don't deserve shit." I will never forget those words from Mark.

On that day, the papers were signed and the attorneys shook hands. I thanked the magistrate for all his help, but something deep down in the pit of my stomach died. From 1999 until 2004, I remained Mark's wife and I thought once the divorce was final that my love for this man would be over.

The love of so many years ago came crashing down throughout every part of my soul, and I cried. No one knew the feeling of sadness I carried with me. I was not able to let it go because not only did I feel the pain but I felt the anger from the pain. The anger I felt for Mark stirred so much in me because this man caused me so much physical pain.

Damien did the same, but I was not in love with Damien. I know all I wanted from Damien was respect and just to know that he knew I was a great person and friend to him. He also caused me so much pain and I will never forget how I stood there begging for help and was left in the middle of the road like a wounded animal.

No one knew, not even Mario, how much sadness I carried with me; although I tried to be so strong, my relationship with Elizabeth became worse. Manuel was no longer living in the apartment with us and it was just her and I. I felt it was time for Elizabeth to be move forward in life on her own. The stress at times was just too much.

Elizabeth was very upset with me one morning as I was speaking to my sister Marcia. She tried to take the phone away from me forcibly. Sadly, a tug of war proceeded and the next thing I remember my little girl was scratching at my face. I was shocked and brokenhearted. This was my child. My child's abusive behavior had finally hit me like a ton of bricks. Since the day Mark left, the cycle of abuse continued to control my life.

From my children to the state trooper the abuse continued on and on.

I found a boarding house and I moved in with several people. The room was a bit expensive but it was in my best interest to get out of the apartment I shared with my daughter. Oh please, do not get me wrong; I love my daughter dearly, through my faith in God I realized that the abuse had never stopped.

I moved to Overbrook Farms. I wanted so much to help the owner of the house. I was the one who did all the cleaning in the house; I cleaned the kitchen, living room and dining room. This woman loved to collect things and I tried to help maintain the house inside and out. I even did so much gardening outside that I ended up with a severe case of poison oak.

I joined the health club and I loved it. This was my only outing. Mario and I continued to date, but as I said before, he had a selfish side. One night, he only had enough money to go to a concert and because he did not have enough for me, he went alone. I was pissed and this is when I knew our relationship was beginning to suffer.

We were companions. Mario had high blood pressure and the medication affected him and our life so much. I became frustrated with the way things had affected us. It had nothing to do with whether I thought he was a great person; it was about the love I thought I needed, but couldn't seem to find. I just wanted to be loved and I know now that I didn't love myself. It wasn't about Mario at all.

Being a part of the gym was wonderful and I started to see a therapist. I was beginning to feel so much better. I really liked my therapist who was just wonderful and finally I was working on me. Then it happened, Elizabeth needed a place to stay and she wanted us to get another place together. I had to call my therapist because all I could do was cry. I knew I did not want to move back with her because I was afraid things would start all over again. I knew the verbal abuse would continue, but all I could do was pray to God that maybe, just maybe, it would be different.

We began looking to rent a house and then Mario suggested I try to get prequalified for a home of my own. I thought, "No way will I be lucky enough to get this loan for my own home." Well it did happen and I was pre-qualified for the loan. I first met with one agent and I could have screamed when she showed me these horrible homes. I then found another agent named Kevin Wheat who became my agent and my friend. It was like talking to an old buddy from years ago.

We went in search of my new home and we found it. It was a beautiful corner house and I fell in love. I made a bid and they accepted my offer. I felt like the queen of the world because I did not need a man to help me with this process. I did this and Elizabeth helped with some of the money, so I was so very grateful to her. Now we would have a roof over our heads and my grandchildren would live in a safe environment.

Before I found this house, I tried to get Manuel to help out so that we would always have a home. Manuel didn't want any part of it; he said that he was not going to allow me or anyone else to ruin his credit. It truly amazes me how much I still tried to help my children and how I continued to allow them to treat me this way.

Elizabeth and I moved in and after we did, Manuel wanted me to make Elizabeth give up her room so he could move in. I said to my loving and wonderful son,

"Son, I tried to get you to agree to help on a bigger house and you refused."

I was not about to kick Elizabeth out of her room when she helped with the house and Manuel had refused. My son carried on for the neighbors and I was cursed and called every name in the book. I watched my children's behavior and realized that they were doing exactly what Mark did; they were trying to control me. It was as though Mark was this great and powerful wiz!!! He was the famous Chief Inspector.

The years of abuse and torment were still haunting me, now through my own children.

I promised that I would never allow my grandchildren to go into a shelter and my daughter knew this, so she used it and she held it over my head. The love I felt for my children and grandchildren was so overwhelming I would not let harm come to them and my daughter knew it.

Yes, many times I would have to kick Manuel out of the house because it would become just too much. There was no respect from either of my children and I was not getting the peace I knew I needed and deserved in my life.

My daughter did not like Mario and she made it a point to speak her mind.

So far, two years have gone by, it was now 2005, and my case against the electric company was ending. I met with a new attorney that the advised me that my case against the state trooper was never filed and time was running out. I was beside myself, and when I asked this new attorney when was he planning on filing, his comment was exactly what the Major had said; "It's your word against his."

Of course, I fired that attorney before I went to the deposition with the electric company and I hired my new attorney. On September 27, 2004, my case against the state trooper was filed.

My new attorney Mr. V, and I went forward with our deposition and we came to a settlement with the electric company.

This pool accident happened to me, but you would think that it had happened to my children. I would have to constantly repeat myself over and over again saying, "You have no right to tell me what to do. This is my money!" I was blessed and so I shared the money with them, but it was never enough.

At times, all children can show a selfish side and can be very ungrateful. Why did I continue to allow my children to punish me? No matter how much I tried to ease any pain of the past, they wouldn't let it go and I continued to remember and live with it too. Many times, I would hear that I needed to get over it. Why was I not able to get over the abuse I sustained? Later on in my life, I finally realized that it was so difficult for me to forget the horrible abuse I went through because I was still living it.

Mario's sister had issues and I believe she always will. I recall the day when his sister called to scold him about introducing me as his girlfriend. She made it quite clear that in the eyes of God I was still Mark's wife and that the divorce didn't matter. How dare she speak about me in this way! Who was she to judge and crucify me?

The memory of my marriage continued to haunt me. My relationship with Mario was not a happy one. I did not care for his sister nor did I want to be in her surroundings. I didn't want to hear her negative comments and I wasn't going to put myself in that situation. I was always polite but that was as far as it went.

I could see right through Mario's sister and I didn't like what I saw. I had suffered enough; her or her family's approval of me didn't matter to me anymore. I didn't have to gain the approval of anyone because I knew I was a decent, loving, compassionate and giving human being.

I attended several family barbecues and Christmas dinners, which were very nice, but I still didn't feel like I belonged. Many family members asked if we were ever going to get married. At first, the answer was yes, but then as time went on, it turned into a no.

From that horrible September day in 2002, I lived in fear and all I wanted was a normal and happy life. I was always afraid the trooper was going to kill me. Many times when I was working out at the gym, I could have sworn I had seen him. I couldn't see the man that looked like him very well since I had my surgeries. My vision was never the same and it was impossible for me to see clearly. Fear would overcome me and I would leave the fitness club in such a panic.

I thought I was so brave when I joined the club and I felt invincible. One morning I was brave enough to take the train into town. It was a great experience and I felt good about it. I was heading back to my home on the Broad Street Subway and a young man around my son's age approached me and asked for a pen. Without thinking, I went into my purse and pulled out a pen and I told the young man that he could keep it because I had plenty. This took place in the afternoon and our Broad Street Subway is always crowded with people, so I felt safe.

This young man then turned around and held the pen like it was a weapon and started leaning into me saying that the way he felt right now he could rob a bank. I was looking directly into his face and I watched as other people also watched. Then from somewhere deep down inside of me, I began to yell at him to go sit down.

I know my big mouth is what saved me and even as my knees were shaking with fear, I was able to pull myself out of the seat and move to a different area of the subway. Until this day, no one will ever be able to convince me that God was not there with me.

One woman asked me if I was all right and I said, "NO." I could not believe everyone was just watching. This horrible feeling took over me and I was so upset I decided right then and there that I would never ride on public transportation again. For years, I kept my promise.

I stopped going to the gym and I hid for quite awhile. Even when I was inside of my home cleaning, I was scared. I never realized how much fear had taken control of my life. The relationship with my son and daughter was horrible. All the anger they built up through the years was being taken out on me.

I thought by buying my children's love it would ease some of the pain. I thought being there for them would help ease the pain of the past, but nothing helped. I would become so frustrated with them because Elizabeth and Manuel would put Mark on a high pedestal.

The police department would call him their golden child. Those who were close to me realized I was covering up something. Even those that were close to Mark were aware that he was abusing me.

Most of my time was spent taking care of our new home. When I think of it now, I know my little family needed so much healing and I just didn't know what to do. I was trying to heal myself and I was not doing such a great job at it. Fighting between Manuel and Elizabeth continued and at times it became physical and I wondered why. It was because of what they saw. I would often wonder if Mark ever realized the damage he had left behind, or did he even care? Did he realize the scars my children and I carried? There has always been a saying, "out of sight out of mind." If you don't see the damage, then it doesn't affect you; it didn't affect Mark at all.

A year or so after my divorce, my son Samuel and daughter Elizabeth said they needed to talk to me and I thought someone was sick. They told me that Mark was getting married; I broke down. I could not believe how knowing that he was going to marry the woman he left home for could hurt so badly. I thought the final blow was when Mark caused me to have retinal detachment surgery. The tears just flowed down my face and the memories of past happy times were all gone. I cried until 5:00am the next morning. Then I stopped crying, perhaps because all the sad memories outweighed the happy memories; the love I once had for Mark was in the past.

I knew my son Manuel was very upset about the wedding because he went wearing jeans, a tee shirt and black boots. My ex mother-in-law was not nice to the children and I guess in her eyes they will always be a bad memory of the truth; a truth they wish would just go away. As much as we try, we can never relive our past. Whether you do right or you do wrong your past life will always be a part of you.

I finally realized that all the sadness that had overwhelmed my children was taking over all of us. How I prayed for an answer and I knew that until we all realized that we needed to get some help, the pain we carry would not go away.

My son Samuel was engaged to Lucy Bonn and I was so happy for him. I thought he would have made an excellent father. Samuel always tried to make peace when it came to his brother and sister. He was my oldest and I always looked to him for moral support.

Maybe Samuel felt I depended on him too much or maybe he was tired of all the constant fighting between his brother and sister. I wish I had the answer to all of my own questions. Sadly, I don't.

My father was getting up in age and they decided to sell the home that he and mom had purchased together. I understood because it was becoming such a stress on Pop and my brother Lee was quite ill. Pop was able to get a very nice small apartment and my brothers Lee and Jose shared an apartment together. I was so happy for them. My father thought I wanted some of the money from the settlement of the house, but the only thing that I wanted was my mother's table, cabinet and dressers. Nothing else really mattered to me; I always felt she was still close by.

As time continued forward, I never had the heart to talk to my family about the horrible abuse I went through because of my shame, guilt and embarrassment. My mother and father loved my husband and they thought the world of him. Before my mother died, she spoke to Mark on the phone. She said to him, "You know what you did was wrong." My mother said he never acknowledged the comment she made and he stayed silent over the phone.

My anger towards my ex- husband continued to build up inside of me and I wanted nothing to do with him. He never invited the children to his home. For all the years of our separation, and even after our divorce, Mark would have the children meet him at a Cousin's Supermarket parking lot or Burger King, or before this year, at Home Depot Parking lot. I still questioned his love and always wondered if he loved these young people as much as they loved him. No matter how angry you may have been at me, they did not deserve to be treated like second-class citizens. What man, what decent man would do the things Mark did? He knew that no matter what, my love for my children was unconditional. No matter how much heartache or sadness was in my heart, I loved my children. My mother always said to me, "You must forgive because if you don't forgive, you will not be able to move on with your life". I use to say, "Mom it's hard, and I feel so much anger." "Carmen, let go of the anger", my mother would say.

Many nights I would cry and many days the memory of all the horrible abuse would not let me move on. I thought I could heal myself; I thought I was strong enough. I stopped going to therapy because I was afraid to get on the bus after my experience on the train; and I just stopped going. Dr. Penny diagnosed me with post-traumatic stress disorder because everything had me on edge.

I was blessed with the greatest neighbors by the names of Cecilia, Renee, and Raheem. Cecilia and I always looked out for one another. We helped each other when it came to the snow and cleaning around the property. Many times we would stand in the back and talk and even on the front porch; we talked about everything and anything. It was great having her as my neighbor. Cecilia was more to me then just my neighbor, she became my sister and I felt blessed. No matter what, we looked out for one another.

Christmas and Thanksgiving would come and go and I promised myself I would do everything in my power to make it a happy one. I made my famous cheesecakes and Raheem loved my cheesecakes and so did Renee. I made it a point to make them their own personal cheesecakes and I baked one for my nephew Lee, who I adored. I always used to say Lee was controlling but I realized later that this wonderful nephew wanted nothing more than to protect me. I loved and appreciated him for that. Our relationship has a strong bond and the love I feel for him is like the love I feel for my own children.

God blessed my nephew with a wonderful family. His longtime girlfriend Leann and three wonderful children by the names of Lourdes, Lee, and Sophia are blessings. My grandchildren, great nieces and nephew were so close and I would watch on many occasions how they would play together. I loved to hear their laughter. WOW! The laughter of a child is just wonderful and to me it is like music.

In November, it was brought to my attention that my son Samuel was not happy in his relationship and sadly, he started dating another woman. No one understood what happened and his fiancée was broken hearted. I couldn't help but feel her pain but I loved my son dearly and I wanted to respect his decision.

The young lady Samuel started dating is a wonderful girl and I loved her too. They attended high school together and they had remained great friends. Samuel wanted my approval, he wanted us to accept her, and we did with open arms because we thought he truly wanted to be with her.

Samuel relocated back to Philadelphia and moved in with us. It was a small three-bedroom house but we tried to make the best of it. I gave up my bedroom because Samuel would wake up at the crack of dawn to get to work and I thought I was doing the right thing.

Rosaura Torres

At first, I would sleep on the sofa and Samuel would sleep in my bed. Then his new girlfriend also started spending the night. I thought it would be for a few nights and then it turned out to be more than just a night or two. I would sleep on the air mattress in our living room, Manuel also moved into our house and we were cramped. Samantha would sleep with me, Jacob would sleep with his mother and Manuel had the front room. Samuel and Maria had my bedroom. We tried to make the best out of a difficult situation.

Samuel and I talked about buying a house where we could all live together as a family in peace. Now Manuel's anger showed its ugly head again. This wonderful hearted young man had so much anger. I am truly sorry I can't answer why my son was so angry. One minute he was happy, but then if you challenged him, he would become quite angry.

At Christmas dinner, my son Manuel showed his anger again and it just broke my heart. He showed no respect and then to make it even worse, it ended with a huge argument.

You know, come to think of it, I could not deal with much of his anger. Everything that would happen caused him to lose his temper. I would ask him to leave. I thought, after constantly telling him to leave he would change his ways, but you know that didn't work either. Manuel moved in with his girlfriend and her mother and everything seemed to be going great, or so I thought.

Now before I go any further, you may be wondering what this has to do with my abuse. The affects of the abuse continued to cause so much drama in our home. It was a nightmare.

Where was my friend Mario through all of this? Well, I was still dating him and I always thought I wanted to get married again. However, I knew marriage was not for me or for Mario.

Samuel found us a new home and we were all very excited. Elizabeth had her doubts and I didn't understand why. She would say, "You two are going to make us feel that this is only your house". We explained to Elizabeth that we are here to support one another and help one another through good and bad.

I remember the day we went to see the house and what a good feeling I had about it this beautiful new place. There were so many people also viewing the property, but a positive feeling came over me and I knew this was going to be our new home.

How excited we were when we put our bid in for the house and they accepted it. Everything was going as planned until we found out that the mortgage company we were dealing with was not putting everything on the table. So many Americans suffered as we did with the sub-prime loan. I already had renters for the first house. My original plan was to sell the house and be out from it. But no, not me, I listened to everyone else and rented my home out to my daughter's friend Iris. At first, I thought they would take care of my home the way I did, but I was in for a horrible surprise.

In the beginning with our new home, we all thought things were going to be different. I didn't realize how difficult it had been for us all and just prayed to move forward with our lives.

Many years had passed since my case was filed against the state and the state trooper for the horrible abuse I survived. For three years in Allentown, Pa., Federal Judge oversaw my case. Month after month and year after year, the attorney for the trooper and the attorneys for the state filed for dismissal after dismissal. My head

Rosaura Torres

felt as though it was going to pop off from all the motions that were filed. I was so amazed when the attorney for Damien wanted me to pay for his attorney fees. What nerve, I couldn't believe any of this.

My father would always say exactly what my mother would say. He wanted me to continue the fight because he said, "You did not deserve to be treated like an animal."

My father took ill in May of 2007, he needed surgery for gallstones, and we all thought he came through it with flying colors. Papi was not taking care of himself well and I had stopped by the hospital to see him. At times, I would talk to my father about the case but I didn't want him to worry about it. I would always say to my father, "Don't worry Papi everything is going to be alright" At times after my mother died I was a bit upset with Pop and I would always tell him that he had to take it easy because it's scary out there. Papi would cater to my two older brothers and my sister. If they needed to go to the clinic, he was there. If they needed to go to the store, he was there. No matter what it was that they needed, Pop was there. I felt it was time someone looked after Dad, so after his surgery I was always at the hospital. After he was released from the hospital, he was sent to a rehab facility to help him get back on his feet. Pop was not as young as he used to be; my father was 87 years old.

Pop did not care too much for the facility and neither did I. I encouraged him and said his stay would only be for a short time. I would call him frequently and I tried to visit him as much as I could. We were always happy to see one another and this was more important to me than anything. He was the only parent I had left and I had made up my mind that no matter what happened I was going to look out for my Pop.

The night before I was planning to attend Mario's family barbecue, my father had a fall. When I arrived at the hospital, I was beside myself. The overwhelming anger and pain I had seeing my father in that condition just left me a complete emotional mess. All I could do was cry and my father kept telling me not to cry. I wanted to know what happened and I wanted an explanation. The doctors at the hospital could only tell me that my father fell at the nursing facility. That was not good enough for me.

The following Monday, I was at the nursing facility and I wanted a full report. I wanted to know who was supposed to be watching my father, and so on. I contacted an attorney, but none wanted to take the case because they felt my father was too old and he would have to go through giving a deposition. I was not surprised by the response I received. Most attorneys only care about one thing and one thing only, money.

The following morning I attended the barbecue and truthfully, I was not in the mood to be there. I was exhausted and all I wanted to do was sleep. Steve and Barbara, were also at the barbecue; they were friends of ours. They helped a lot to pick up my mood and I was grateful that they were there.

Pop healed okay but then I noticed that he was bending over more than usual and the nursing facility released him in this condition anyway. I believed in my heart he was going to be fine. The day my father was released, my daughter Elizabeth and I went to visit him at his apartment. When we saw the condition he was in, it left my daughter and I extremely shaken up. Elizabeth and I took my father, put him in the bath, and bathed him. At no time was I embarrassed with seeing my father nude, I had to care for him.
All I could think about was that I wanted my father to get well and I was going to make sure he got back to the

hospital. Having Elizabeth there to help me meant more than I could ever express to her. Pop was admitted back into Our Lady of Lourdes Hospital. Mario and I traveled almost every day back and forth to see him. No matter what, I was there. I realized this was important to him, so I took over power of attorney. I didn't want my siblings to fight the way they had when my mother died. This was not the time for fighting. We may not have always agreed on things, but we were still a family.

During the time of my father's illness, my oldest son Samuel did not keep up with his responsibilities. We all knew that he started cheating on his new girlfriend. Most people would say to mind your own business and I tried, but what I didn't expect was my son to bring his affair into my world. I was his mother and all I wanted was for the family to be there for one another. My son Samuel had not been paying the bills. Right before I was to head out to New Jersey to see my father, my electric was shut off. I couldn't believe any of this, this was my son and he made it quite clear to me what was more important to him. My relationship with my son was extremely strained. I didn't want my father to know any of this horrible nonsense was taking place at home. I borrowed money from my nephew to turn the electric back on and went on as usual, trying to take care of Pop. Through the months, Pop was in and out of the hospital. My son Samuel came to see my father but my father never knew what was going on at home. He said to me, "Daughter, your son does not love you the way a son should love his mother". I looked over at my father and I asked him, "Why you would say that Papi?" and he said, "Because I can see it." I never questioned Pop again; I just went on as usual. Drama after drama continued in my home. Maria finally caught Samuel in the act; it was like an episode of "Cheaters". Poor Maria, my heart went out to her. I'm sure she never dreamed he would do this to her. As much as I love my son, I knew he was going to do the same to her as he did to Lucy. I just prayed time and time again that I was wrong.

On a Sunday evening, I received an email from my attorney. The federal judge that was overseeing the case wanted us to prepare for our discovery and he wanted discovery to take place on Monday. I received a phone call from my attorney telling me that the trooper's attorney made an offer. I could not believe the offer they made me or how they said this was just a personal injury case. I also couldn't believe how they continued to ignore the horrible abuse I went through. My God, I was not an attorney, but I knew this was domestic violence.

The Judge from Federal Court had scheduled the trial to begin on July 17th and there was a rush for discovery. Deposition was scheduled for each day. The Major on Monday and Trooper Sob were scheduled for Friday.

I made it quite clear to my attorney I was not going to settle and that I wanted to go to trial. He wanted to know how much I thought the case was worth, but it was not about the money. Did my own government truly forget how horrible and brutally I was hurt? Could they ever imagine the horror I went through and continue to live through? No one could truly understand the affect domestic violence has had on so many like me; not until they walk in our shoes. They were trying to dismiss me as if I was an animal. I even pulled over for a defenseless animal many years ago and this man left me there, begging for help. I will never truly understand how another human being could do this to me; he just left me there defenseless. I would pray to God and ask him repeatedly, "Why?"

All day on Monday, all I could do was cry as I tried to understand how my government could ignore what this trooper did to me. I got myself together and the next morning I received a phone call from my attorney. The judge from Allentown, PA wanted to meet with the defendant and myself with our attorneys. I said that would be just fine but I was not going to settle and I wanted to go to trial. Mr. V said, "Yes Carmen, I know. But we must be there."

The following morning I was an emotional wreck. Our ride to Allentown was not so great, I was so sick to my stomach. Mario stopped at the nearest drug store to purchase some an-acid for me, but that didn't even help. We arrived before my attorney did and I was just a buddle of nerves. Mario and Maria tried everything possible to ease my anxiety. We talked about everything except the case. I was truly grateful that they were there with me trying to ease my mind.

After about 45 minutes, all the suits came out and then I was directed to the conference room where my attorney was waiting for me. At first his conversation went like this, "Carmen the state feels that they have made a thorough investigation". My response to him was, "Oh yeah, well, they made a thorough investigation into covering it up." I was not going to sit there much longer; I could feel my blood pressure rising. Mr. V, said, "Carmen, just wait, just wait, let me tell you what happened." I calmly waited as Mr. V explained to me the outcome of their meeting. It turns out that because the trooper, Damien, was detailed to Harrisburg, PA at the time that I was brutally assaulted, he was held responsible for the injuries I sustained and he was liable. I could not believe my ears and the next words Mr. V said to me was, "Carmen, God is with you." I replied, "All the time". Through all of the horrible abuse I sustained, I knew that God was with me through all of it and I continued to believe.

We left the conference room and went into Judge Paul's court room, the charges were dropped against Coronal Moore and Damien's other commander and my case was now pushed back to where the abuse took place. The ruling came down on June 6, 2007. I felt like I was coming closer to the end of my nightmare. The next day, Mario and I went to visit my father and I told him all the great news. So many years waiting to hear from Judge Paul and finally he found the evil trooper liable for the injuries I had suffered.

Pop was so happy for me and I told him that once this case was over and done, and no matter what the outcome was, he would come to live with me. I was going to make sure he would get back on his feet. My dream of my father coming to live with me did not turn out the way I had planned. My father's health became worse and he was then transferred from the hospital to the nursing facility. That was until one day my father begged his doctor to come home with me, and I said, "YES".

My father was bedridden, he was on a feeding tube and he was not able to walk anymore. Pop could not even hold his head up the way he wanted to. Many times Papi would talk about the foods he loved to eat and it broke my heart. I was taught by the nurses at the hospital how to clean his feeding tube, how to feed him, check his sugar and to clean his catheter. I remember calling Direct Television to provide him with more Spanish stations but my Pop just wanted his usual stations. The first night was difficult; Pop could not sleep and he kept talking to himself. I thought I would go up to my bedroom and get a few hours of sleep. Sadly, the night didn't go as I had planned. I heard my father calling me so I remained on the sofa on his side. My father became worse and over the weekend, I called my cousin Jim to meet me at Frankford Hospital. Because Dad was really at his worst, the doctor wanted to admit him into the hospital to inject a larger IV into his neck. Dad had already gone through this horrible procedure and I knew this was not going to help him. You see, Pop came home to die and he wanted to die next to me. During the short time he was with us, my daughter Elizabeth helped me clean him. I remember my Pop would beg Elizabeth to heal him please.

We cried as Mario helped the nurses with Pop as we tried to roll him over. I am thankful for them being by my side. The visiting nurse came by to see Dad that Sunday and she said, "It is time to take your father to Hospice care." I wanted more than anything to hold on to what was left of my Pop; I just couldn't accept taking him to Hospice, but I knew it was for the best. You see, through the all my sadness, my daughter and I became extremely close.

Pop would not let me leave him nor was I planning on leaving him so I traveled with my father to Holy Redeemer Hospital. Even on his first day there, I felt a sense of peace. I made sure he was settled in and I told him I would be back the following day with my bag and I would be staying with him. My father was admitted into St. Joseph's Manor on Sunday evening and from that time on, I only spent one night at my home. I would sleep on the sofa and the nurses would come and look for me because my father wanted me. Pop would say, "Where were you"? I would tell him, "I am right here Papi, I am not going to leave your side". My uncle Jim came from Puerto Rico and my Dad was surrounded by his family.

One Friday, my son Samuel came to visit his grandfather with his new girlfriend and I was not very happy about it. Their relationship had caused so much drama that I was not in the mood for them to visit at that time. The only reason I never lost my temper was because the girlfriend came with her daughter. Pop was asleep and he never remembered seeing her.

In the short week that I spent with my father while caring for him, we would watch his favorite Spanish soap opera. I have to laugh about this now because Pop would blast the volume so loud and he would tell me, "I am going to walk out of here." I would agree with him because my father had such a strong will to live, it was amazing. I believed in my heart that a miracle would happen and he would be well again.

This truly breaks my heart to say this but, my sister Edwina, as usual, was having some financial problems and she wanted some money from Dad on his death bed. My sister and two older brothers were in the hospital asking for money. I couldn't believe it when I was told by the staff. I was pissed beyond anything you can imagine. My father told me to give her the money and because I respected my father's wishes, I gave her it to her. I would be a liar if I didn't say how angry I was with my sister and two brothers. I realize this was not about them. Pop was always there for them and I loved and respected my father, so I abided by his decision.

The night before my father passed, we were watching television and he asked me to call my aunt Liza because he saw on the Spanish station a commercial that could help heal him. He wanted my Aunt to come get him so I called her and she calmed him down.

Pop would make me look at his legs and say, "Look, I can move them". I would say to Pop, "You sure can". I did not nor was I ever going to discourage my father and I kept all the hope up for him. I would hold his hand and tell him repeatedly how much I loved him and how lucky I was to have him in my life. He would often say he was not a good father; but I would say, "You're wrong, you are a wonderful father. Papi you were there, through the good and through the bad, you were always there for us Pop."

It was on that same Saturday that my father looked at me and said, "Don't worry Carmen, you're going to win, you have to continue the fight and don't give up". I said, "Pop, please do not worry about my case, I just want you to get better."

Maybe I was not being truthful to myself because after Sunday's visit and everyone was gone, Mario and I were sitting on the sofa in the family room. I dozed off for just a minute and I saw my father's face flash in front of me. I said to Mario, "I have to go check up on my father". I went into the room and I looked at him and said, "Papi!" I kept saying his name as I walked over to him and laid my hand on his chest. It was then that I felt the last beat of my father's heart; he was gone.

I thought I was ready for my father to go home with my mother; I was not. I couldn't believe the scream I heard from my voice and all I could do was cry. I held my father's hand; he was still warm and I did not want to let him go. My sons and daughter came before the funeral home took him and they were able to say good-bye to their grandfather. I knew my father was dying; I arranged his funeral even before his death. I just did not want to believe it was going to happen.

Our beloved father was a wonderful man. He always provided for us and always made sure that there was food on the table and a roof over our heads. Our father was there for all of his children and all of their different needs. When my sister Edwina was a little girl, she remembers there was not a car available to take her to the hospital. Our father took her to the hospital by piggyback. Up until the day, his time came to go home with our mother; he still worried about the safety of his children. My sisters and brothers feel that we were blessed to have two strong and positive parents in our lives. If I continue to talk about all the good memories we have about our father, I could go on forever...

This was the memoriam written by my cousin Jim:

A TRUE UNCLE

My uncle Jesus was a person who had such an impact on my life. At 51, I still see him towering over me as a boy, and always talking about different things.

When I was a young boy, I remember sleeping over a lot and hanging out with my cousins. To me he was a great leader, who lead by example and would tell you what he thought was correct whether you liked it or not.

I can remember we would always drive to New York to see a big screen movie, understand that at age 9, that screen was big. He would take me to the movies, and then we would have dinner. It was always spaghetti and meatballs, which I loved in a small restaurant in New York. Imagine watching BEN HUR for the first time on a gigantic screen. It was great!

We would always watch wrestling, roller derby and go to the matches at the arena on 46th and Market St. I remember going every week with him it sure seemed like that. He always was providing for his kids; they had to be number one or he was not content that day.

My uncle used to wear a hat, a real character he was when he wanted to be. He would pack the car with all of us and take us to the lake, shopping or anywhere WE WANTED TO GO. He would always ask his kids, "want to come", whether the car was full or not. I am sure that for all who knew and loved him, he will be missed. I understand now that if it was not for his positive and tremendous influence in my life, I don't know where I would be now.

Thank you, Lord, for giving me an Uncle like Jesus.

The Obituary:
Written by Jim Ortiz, Jr.

Jesus I. Ortiz was born on June 6, 1919, in Yakama, Puerto Rico. He was the oldest child of five born to the late Steven and Esther Ortiz.

He met and fell in love and married Isabella De La Rosa. From this union came eight children, Anna Jordon, Lee, Jr. Ralph, Edwina, Marcia, Arturo and Carmen. They were blessed to share a long, fun, exciting and sometimes-interesting life together until my mother Isabella went home on July 3, 2003.

Jesus continued his life until illness slowed his pace. He finally settled at Ferry Avenue Station and then relocated to the Philadelphia PA area with his daughter Carmen. It was a short stay, until he relocated to St. Joseph Manor, in Huntingdon Valley. On Sunday evening, September 9 around 10:45 pm, Jesus was called home to take his resting place beside his wife Isabella.

He leaves to cherish his memories three sons, Jordon, Lee, Jr. and Ralph; three daughters, Edwina, Marcia and Carmen one brother Jim Sr.; one sister-in-law, Linda; one nephew, Jim, Jr.; nieces Maida and Gloria; 13 grandchildren; thirteen great-grandchildren.

On September 9, 2007, my father went home with my mother. The services were beautiful and everyone was

Rosaura Torres

so happy with how I handled everything. My daughter and Maria made food and I was blessed to have them with me in my time of need. My father looked so handsome and finally at peace. My heart was so heavy and I felt so much pain. After Papi died, I was not myself, I cried more and more and I felt like I was losing my grip on life. My children made the comment that I was losing my mind and I felt my entire world was crumbling around me.

One afternoon I thought my world would never be the same, my mother father were both gone; how would I go on? I just didn't know what to do and I felt so lost. The dark hole that overwhelmed my life for all these years was starting to swallow me whole again.

Rosaura Torres

IV

I came across a web site called Abuse of Power and I began to read. I could not believe the things that took place involving city and state police as well as the Military. For years now, many city and states officers and even military persons had abused their power, time and time again. Domestic Violence is very high in this line of work and what makes this so outrageous is how they use their positions to get away with the abuse. They are able to speak to the District Attorney's in the city courts and to the judges. Many judges have given these great men in blue protection orders from abuse because they don't believe they would lie. After all, they are the law.

I took the time, I reached out to Ms. D. I began to tell her my story. All I could do was cry because I realized I never took the time to get the help I needed. Since the horrible abuse, I sustained from my husband and then from the state trooper, I thought I could heal myself. I was so wrong. Ms. D. felt I should reach out to someone in the Philadelphia area and meet with other women who have been through abuse similar to what I had been through, so, I did.

I looked into Women against Abuse and I was not so sure about them. I am not trying to offend the organization, but sadly, I was not pleased. Then I came upon Women in Transition. I met with my counselor Hero. Several of my visits involved me breaking down and crying. This wonderful lady gave me the strength to meet with other women and this is when my journey toward recovery began. It is amazing how the time goes by and how lucky I am to have met all of these great women: Marie, Rene, May, LA and Kat had suffered just as I did. Month after month and group after group I became aware of how great I was beginning to feel. I no longer blamed myself for the horrible abuse that took place in my life. I was beginning to love myself.

I would be a liar if I didn't tell you that I still have fear of fighting against the State of Pennsylvania and against this sad, pathetic man. Would he come after me one day? I often wonder if this will ever happen.

During my time of healing, I waited patiently for my case to move forward and I realized that I am not the only one that feels negatively about our court system. They try to ignore the injustice by officers of the law and many of us victims of domestic violence. We became a very close group of women and we looked out for one another. Even after our group sessions, we always kept in touch with one another during the week.

I would send my attorney email after email wanting to see the outcome of my case. I wanted to know when we were supposed to go to trial. A year came and went and I heard nothing. He never had answers for me except for the same old reply; he's "waiting for the State Attorney General." The most amusing thing happened one day I was standing waiting for Mario to pick me up from one of my group session when I noticed the assistant state attorney general was walking by. I remember shaking her hand when I was in federal court; I would see her often and she would turn and smile. I would smile back never saying anything until one day I was in the elevator

with her and I got up the courage to speak. I said, "You don't remember me?" She replied. "No, sorry I don't". I looked at her and I said, "I'm Carmen Stun." We chatted for a bit and I was proud to say I now belonged to "Women in Transition". She had this particular look on her face and all she said was, "Good luck."
I saw her several times but we never spoke again. As the months continued forward the love and support I received from my sisters and my supporters was a blessing.

Mr. V. informed me he had scheduled the deposition for the "evil one", (that's what I call him), Damien, the state trooper.

With the help of "Women in Transition," I was able to finally speak to my ex husband after almost ten years. It was time to forgive. You see, Mark retired from the Philadelphia Police Department and everyone said he would be the next police commissioner of Philadelphia, but I knew different.

There were too many skeletons in his closet, many people knew of the horrible abuse and his leaving me not even a month after my surgery. Yes, I was abandoned, and now I can say it was a blessing. When it happened back then, I didn't feel so blessed; but, of course, I do now.

Mark was one of my abusers and until he can make peace with himself, he will never be able to live in his own skin. I am a constant memory of the past. You can move on and become the Chief of Police in another city. You can even try to act as if you never had another family, but it's just not possible to change the truth.

Poor Mark, he even thought I was going to speak to the newspaper where he was now the new Chief of Police in the little town where I was severely injured. Of all the places for Mark to become the new Chief of Police, he chose the same town where the state trooper had abused and abandoned me.

My anger for Mark was gone, I will always remember the abuse he put me through and I am sure he will always remember me cheating on him. No matter what, the memory of the abuse will live with me for the rest of my life. I made it quite clear to Mark that I had no intention to speak to the newspaper; I wanted to make peace and move on. My mother always said I had to forgive because if I didn't forgive I would not have been able to move on. Mark made sure that I received my part of the pension and I was grateful for all his help.

When I think of how much it cost me, no money in the world will ever return my vision back to me. No money in the world would remove the scars of so many years ago!

I'm sure many would like for me to keep silent and to stop voicing the horrible truth behind the badge! I know I have ruffled many feathers but I refuse to keep silent.

Many officers all over the United States and I am sure throughout the country continue to abuse their power!

Whether it is from racial profiling, to police brutality or domestic violence, this abuse of power is a serious matter within all Police Departments.

Many have hidden behind the badge and many feel they are justified for the pain they have inflicted on so many innocent people. I happen to be one of them!

For years, others would hide the truth and continue to hide what really happened. But, the abuse of the past is shining through the dark hole of sorrow and despair.

You cannot hide; you cannot lie. The truth does come out in the end.

I did my own investigation and I asked Mark if Lt. Moore was still on the police department and he was not. I even asked Mark about police procedure and I made my poor ex husband uncomfortable. Now, he did tell me that I should settle, and I said, "No. This is about more than just the money; this is how my own government ignored the horrible abuse one of their officers did to another human being. I have never threatened this man and I will never wish him any harm."

Then it finally hit me, Mark could care less about what happened to me, he was more concerned about his own ass. He did not want the City of Lancaster to know he abused his ex-wife.

On two separate occasions, the deposition was rescheduled and my stress level was reaching its boiling point. I remember entering my group, breaking down, crying, and telling them how the State's Attorney General had rescheduled it once again. This was on a Wednesday, my spirit was extremely low, and the deep sorrow I felt in the past seemed to be coming back to me again.

The following day, my depression got the best of me. It's true, once the negative energy takes a hold of you it's hard to let go. I fell asleep on my sofa and I awoke as thought I pulled a muscle. I was not feeling well and I took myself right up to bed. From Thursday afternoon until Sunday morning, my condition became worse and Mario came directly from his job and took me to the hospital. I could not understand what was wrong with me; it was so difficult for me to breath. The doctors asked if I smoked which I do not. I was in so much pain and I just didn't understand what was going on with my body. The doctor's ran several tests and the results were that I had phenomena and I was diagnosed with diabetes. I could not believe any of this, although I knew my parents had it as they became older. I had horrible nightmares while I was in the hospital. This new diagnosis saddened my heart even more and I prayed to God each day, I would do everything in my power to take better care of myself. The priest visited me and with so much patience, he took the time to come and pray over me. He asked me when the last time was that I attended church and I was not going to lie to the priest. It had been years and I could not help to express how I felt. I said I had more faith in God than most people who go to church every Sunday.

I don't think he was too amused with my comment but with that, he smacked the paper on my forward and I could smell the nicotine on his breath. Before the priest started to pray, I told him he needed to stop smoking. The father said his prayers and left. I even asked my sister May who is Muslim, to pray for me. We believe in one GOD and I believe our God always heard her.

Many must wonder if I am bitter about the abuse I endured for many years of my young adult life. I am not bitter; I am free of the abuse; not only physical but the mental and the emotional pain I suffered by my abusers.

For years I would hear, "I am sorry", and "It won't happen again!" as well as, "If you report this, I will lose my job on the police department!"

I sacrificed myself to protect another human being who did not protect me! My sister and I spoke on how difficult it has been to move forward because of the memories of the abuse. I have moved forward. Why am I speaking out and telling my story? So many women, children and men are suffering because of Domestic Violence. I want to let them know, that they are special, wonderful, awesome, dynamic people!

I prayed for years that my abuser would say, "I'm sorry" or "I'm sorry for what I did!", or perhaps even, "I'm sorry for causing you to have eye surgery, I'm sorry for the pain I inflicted on you!" ... I'm sorry for everything!"

I never heard any of those words and I never will. I no longer wait to hear "I'm sorry." I am at PEACE. My question to my abusers is: Will you ever find PEACE? I pray that you do because no matter where you are, the abuse you caused will always be a part of you and your legacy.

I received a phone call from my oldest brother Lee and I cried like a baby, and he said, "Hey sis, please stop crying. It's going to be all right." The next day my brother came to visit me and since that day, I have become very close to him. My brothers' positive energy flowed through him into me and he had the faith I needed to get through all of this. I began to use it because I believe that as long as you have faith in God, he will help you through anything.

Sadly, my sons were angry and I did not see them while I was hospitalized. My daughter Elizabeth made sure she visited with my grandchildren. However, Elizabeth at times could be a pain in my butt. I love my children and for years, I carried this horrible shame. The shame of not protecting my children weighed heavily on my soul. The horrible abuse they had to witness and the sadness it caused invaded my family.

At first, I was so upset with my sons for not visiting me and then I realized that they would have to make peace with themselves. I was not able to help them any further. All I could do for my sons was to continue to love them, and that is what I have done.

I tried repeatedly to save our home. My income was just not enough. I realized I would have to move and give up the house. Elizabeth was in school to be a phlebotomist and for three nights a week, I was with my grandbabies. I promised my daughter that no matter how bad things would get between us or how much arguing we did, I would always stick by her side. I had no more time in my life to argue with my daughter or sons. It was time to move forward, and no matter what, the love I have for my children will always be there.

In November 2008, my group sisters and I graduated from "Women in Transition". This was one of the happiest days of my life. My group sisters were my support system. Through the crying and through my illness, they were there for me. My Advocate's were those wonderful, positive and loving Women.

I, together with five of my group sisters: Marie, Rene, May, LA and Kat and our wonderful counselor and advocate Hero, created a quilt in honor of our advocates. This was to help them move forward as victims and survivors of Domestic Violence. Our memory and work will live on for many years to come through this quilt.

In February, I relocated to a small one-bedroom apartment. My daughter Elizabeth and her boyfriend Lance along with my granddaughter Samantha and grandson Jacob moved into a house. It is located in one of the worst neighborhoods in Philadelphia, PA, but Elizabeth continued with her classes in the medical field. My peace with my sons came and I cannot begin to tell you how grateful I am to the Almighty for the positive blessings he has given me.

We've all been through some rough patches but I will never give up on my children or myself. Never did I give up believing in the justice system and never will I give up on receiving justice for myself one day.

Elizabeth went through some rough times these last couple of months but I have always told her, "Don't give up! We are going to be fine." Elizabeth finished school and she did her externship at Germantown Hospital. Her boyfriend Lance also did his internship at Pennsylvania Hospital and he was offered a position. I am so proud of them both.

Elizabeth told me repeatedly that I would always come to the rescue and she thanked me for all my help. I am so proud of my children. My heart is filled with joy.

Mario and I are living together now. He still has a lot to learn about women, as many men do. He was never in a long lasting relationship until the last six years that we have been together. I have never cheated on him; there was no need. He was not abusive and I would not allow him to talk down to me or degrade me. Yes, we might have some strong words and he is still trying to get used to my overwhelming need for neatness. However, the love and respect we have for each other is very important to us both.

I became a member on the social networking sites not because I wanted to meet people, but I realized many newspapers and other media stations would not write my story. This is when I decided that no one would be able to write my story better than I could, so here you have it.

There have been so many wonderful and outstanding heroes in my life: people such as Cloud-writer, Terri, Anthony and so, many, many more.

The horrible feeling of being alone is gone; I know now more than ever that I have so many outstanding people at my side.

I was blessed to have found two wonderful extended family members from my past and I felt that now, as an Activist against Domestic Violence, I would be able to help them. Star and Tim are the two wonderful people I lost so many years ago and they never knew what happened to me over the years.

More than 20 years have passed and I often questioned my self-confidence. Why was my self-esteem so low? Why did I feel my worth was zero? During my marriage, I felt like whatever I did it was never enough; that no matter what I did as a wife, as a partner or as a friend, it was never enough. I could not explain that each and every time my ex-mother-in-law would visit it was as if I was under a microscope and it made me a nervous wreck.

I always wondered if my cooking or my cleaning was ever good enough for her to accept me. Accepting any position in my life should have been enough. Not until recently did I finally realize that this family was completely full of negativity. If you did not hold a title or you were not a light skin black person, you were not accepted. I didn't understand how being a Latina woman was negative. It was because I was not from their side of the street.

I watched as my ex-mother-in-law and her long time friend Pam interfered in two young people's lives. I saw the love Star and Tim had for one another, but my ex-mother in law and Pam were just too blind to see what I witnessed.

In the end, this young couple went their separate ways. This wonderful young woman married a man who did nothing but abuse her. The memories of the abuse Star endured lives with her unto this day. Star's life continued to spiral downhill. She felt blessed to have three wonderful children, but her heart will always

Rosaura Torres

belong to Tim. You may wonder why it was not possible for this wonderful couple to come together.

Tim suffered two horrible marriages. He was also blessed with two children. He never found the love he lost so many years ago.

Mark's family constant meddling caused chaos time and time again. I finally realized that they were not happy with themselves. It was important for them to interfere in other people's lives and to bring misery and pain to the people they claimed to love.

For years, I felt like a failure and now I know it was not me. It didn't matter what position my ex-husband held on the police department or any police department for that matter. The memory of the abuse I endured by his hands will live with him for the rest of his life. I have no ill will for him or the other abusive relationships I was involved in. I only pray that one day they will come to terms with what they did to me, so that they too can find peace.

No abuser will ever be able to live in his own skin until he or she is able to make peace with themselves and their victim(s).

Now, I do not allow them to anger me as I did so many years ago. I pity their ignorance and their small, closed minds. I pray that one day they will be able to make peace with themselves. I am at peace and I know what a remarkable woman I am. I will NOT hold on to the title of a victim until it's time for me to go home. I am a Survivor.

I continued to move forward for justice, and through the years, never knowing how our justice system will handle this case. In the past seven years, I have tried to tell my story of abuse to several of our Pennsylvania State

225

Senator's. One of my state senator's told me there was not much he could do because this was now a civil tort case. I've contacted The United States Justice Department and every news media, television and newspaper; no one wanted to print my story.

Is it because he was a State Trooper? What was it? Could it be because it was a domestic violence abuse issue? Many questions continue to weigh on my mind. Is it because I am a Latina?

On September 30, 2008, the trooper gave his deposition and my attorney gave me a copy. This so-called man of the law lied repeatedly. He lied. I begged for help. He lied and said the emails were not his; he lied repeatedly. What frustrates me with this entire case is, our government allowed this horrible trooper to retire from the department at the age of 48 so he could keep his pension.

Year after year, I would contact my attorney because there have been numerous times when he would not speak to me or return any of my calls. I was frustrated with him with and his lack of compassion. I needed him to advocate for me. I will not deny nor hide the fact that many times I wished he would just quit. I tried to reach out to other attorney's but they would not take my case. They would tell me that the case has been too long in the justice system. Shit! Who are we kidding? They would not get a large amount of the settlement and that is why they would not take my case.
This had nothing to do with me receiving justice; it has to do with money these attorneys' would have to accept, what little money they would receive in return!

I would see cases come and go, police involved in domestic violence. Their boyfriends and husbands who were police, state police and military officers were killing woman after woman. Many of my sister's have died by the hands of so many men of the law.

Many times my emotional state of mind was quite difficult and sad. I know there is a GOD; I received so much positive support from family and friends and my supporters from "Women in Transition". I received support from everyone I now know, except for one of my brothers, who is a very negative man and has never had faith in the rest of his siblings. My brother is just a very judgmental, critical, and negative person. Recently I was offered the opportunity to have a one woman show on the radio in an effort to tell my story. I was beside myself with excitement. I was sharing my excitement with my brother and he laughed at me. My brother's opinion was that I was not the only victim of abuse by the hands of police officers and it was no big deal. I couldn't believe I would hear these words from my own brother.

As an activist against domestic violence, I can speak on the horrible issues that affect so, many women, children and men who are suffering and will continue to suffer.

This is my story, this is my life, this horrible abuse cost me my vision. I will speak out on this. I feel sorry for my brother, maybe this is why I refuse to call him as much as I use too. He too, needs many prayers.

As I sit here patiently, waiting to go to trial, I still can't understand why my own government has ignored my case. Never did they follow their own procedures and policies within the state police. Never was this trooper reprimanded, disciplined or even brought up on charges for the horrible abuse I sustained seven years ago.

My biggest mistake was that I didn't speak out about the abuse that lasted for 16 years of my marriage much sooner.

To my ex-husband: My soul, my spirit, my body meant nothing to you. I pray one day you will be able to find the peace you so desire.

I could leave this world tomorrow but my memory will live on through my children, grandchildren and my brothers and sisters. To those wonderful ladies at my apartment complex: Thank you for always laughing with me through one of the roughest times in my life.

We have been blessed with a new President named Barack Obama and a wise Latina United States Supreme Court Justice named Sonia Sotomayor.

Mario and I are proud to say that with his parents as well as his sister Aida and her husband, we were blessed to watch as our 44th President of the United States was sworn in as the first African American President. I listened with tears flowing down my cheeks on that cold day looking up at the Washington Monument. On that day, I believed in positive change for this country and this is why I will not give up on receiving justice for my ordeal.

Each night I pray for strength and each night I truly believe that God is giving me the strength to move forward.

I am extremely happy to tell you that my attorney has filed a motion to begin trial and I am ecstatic because we are near an end. Or so, I thought...

I need to share with you that just recently my ex-husband's sister-in-law demanded that Star not speak to me any further because she called me a liar. I feel pity for her and for those who continue to try to cover the lies that they tell to keep the secret of her brothers' abuse towards me.
I wrote this small paragraph for Delia:

Rosaura Torres

Many years ago while I was an administrative assistant for a security company, a certain person realized I was being abused and in order to protect her loved one, she handed me a plane ticket to Chicago to visit my brother. Her name is Star.

Just recently, I was blessed to have found Star on a social website. I lost contact with her for more than 10 years. We decided that no matter what took place in the past we would continue to have love and support for each other.

Star was also a victim of Domestic Violence. My ex-husband's sister shipped me off to Chicago and now she is trying to force Star not to speak to me.

The lies of the past will always interfere with our future. I was called a liar for talking about what happened to me so many years ago. Well, it did happen!

As I said before, one can forgive and I have forgiven, but I will never be able to forget.

To my ex family member, I feel sadness for you and pity. I wish you nothing but the best. I pray that one day you will find peace in your heart, because I have!

To all my wonderful friends and family, thank you for all your love and support. It means the world to me. From you I get my strength and my courage.

The love and strength that flows through me is remarkable and I know that no matter what my past abusers or their families did, they will never be able to hurt me again. I am strong and blessed. Let me end my story with these final thoughts:

Ten years have passed since my first surgery. For years, I went into hiding never feeling safe. Domestic violence has overwhelmed my life and has frightened me time and time again.

With the love and support from my children, group sisters, and advocates and my wonderful friends, their continued encouragement has brought me out of hiding.

No money in the world would ever be able to replace my vision. I am no longer the woman that worked for Al' Dia' Newspaper and I am no longer the woman who could get behind the wheel of her car and go and help others as they have helped me.

I am a woman who refuses to keep the code of silence! I am a woman who will move forward for justice not only for me, but also for all women who have suffered and continue to suffer from abuse.

The strong, positive and determined woman I have become today continues to have my own personal nightmares.

Moving on from domestic violence is not so easy to do. My abusers cost me my vision. Each morning I wake up and I am reminded of what was left behind after my surgery and the young woman who was left behind in the middle of the road.

I know now our God has protected me for a reason. I am one of the lucky ones. YES, I am a survivor of domestic violence. My determination and strength flows through me from my mother and father and I will help others. To my abusers I say this, "I am still here and blessed because I can SPEAK OUT AGAINST DOMESTIC VIOLENCE."

Thank you all for your love and support.

To those who laughed, judged and crucified me. I pray for you, everyday.

I continue moving forward for justice and will return one day to share with you the outcome of justice served.

With all my love and support,

Carmen De La Rosa

V

I am including several of my blogs from the past year:

FORGIVENESS FOR THE PAST

Tonight I had a wonderful conversation with a loving, wonderful friend. We spoke of the lost years. We spoke how Domestic Violence has affected our lives.

Domestic Violence is an epidemic that is completely out of control in our Country and all over the world. My abusers were law enforcement officers. They abused their power. No one is above the law. My memory of the past has lived with me for many years. I was told numerous times no one will ever listen to my cry for help and no one did until I stood up for myself.

Many years ago, I was attending a Spanish banquet and a female officer who I have known for years came to warn me my abuser was going to do everything in his power to have me arrested and because of this warning, I fled the city.

To all victims of Domestic Violence, stand up, keep your head high and do not be afraid anymore. You have rights; your voice will be heard!

Rosaura Torres

You're not alone anymore and never believe that because of the position your abuser holds as a city, state, or military officer, they do not have the right to abuse you!

Many survivors are free from the abuse, but they are not free from the lasting memories of what happened to them. My children and I have moved forward because of the love and support we have given to one another.

Many family members continue to lie about the abuse of the past. My mother and father before their death would say to me, "Carmen, continue the fight because you deserve better; you did not deserve to be abused." This is why I continue to speak out against domestic violence!

God is on my side.

God bless all victims and survivors of Domestic Violence.

OUT OF THE DARKNESS, INTO THE LIGHT

I must emphasize my interviews are to tell the truth of what happened to me so many years ago. We, as survivors, must not and should not continue to protect our abusers. My mistake was that I did protect one of my abusers and in the end, it cost me to have retinal detachment from the right eye.

My silence could have cost me my life, but I survived. I put my trust into another abuser and he felt that what he did to me was justifiable. This cost me retinal detachment from the left eye.

I saw the light and my inner spirit and the strength from my parents is the reason why I fought back! I refuse to take blame for the horrible abuse I endured so many years ago.

Therefore, to those who may be offended or wish I would continue to keep the silence, I out-right refuse. I survived and I am truly blessed because I now will be able to help those who were afraid to speak out about their abuse.

God bless all of the survivors and victims of Domestic Violence. To those abusers, look out because I will be standing by and standing strong for those who feel they are alone! You are not alone; I am here!

With much respect and love,

Carmen De La Rosa

TO MY ABUSERS

Can I change the pain of the past? Can I run from the memories of the past? No, I cannot! I tried and it was not the answer.

Now, to my past abusers can you run and hide from the damage that you have caused? No matter where you go in life, the memory of the abuse you caused me will be following each step you take.

Have you ever sat down and thought to yourself, my god what have I done? I am supposed to protect the woman, child or man that I love. Why is it so difficult for you to be remorseful for the pain you have caused?

To all abusers, you cannot run nor can you hide from the abuse that you have inflicted on so many victims.

I pray each night that, my past abusers will find peace. Because of their denial and lies, it will be difficult for them to find peace of mind.

My peace shines brightly through me; I feel like I can climb the highest mountain and scream out loud and thank God for bringing so many wonderful people into my life.

I will not hide. I will not be afraid. I am strong and positive. I will speak out and I will continue for justice because I am on the right side of the law.

Even after I have gone home, I know that my memory will live on through my children and grandchildren and great, great grandchildren and all my wonderful friends and family!

So, to all of you...thank you again for all of your love and support!

Carmen De La Rosa

MY CHILDREN

From the very beginning that my children moved inside me, I was frightened. What type of mother would I be?

More than anything, I wanted my babies to be happy, to feel safe, to be proud of themselves. Through the years of Domestic Violence, I felt I failed my children. I let them see a sad, weak, and at times, a very depressed mother.

I am writing this short note again because of them! Their love and support through all my pain has brought me out of the darkness.

To my oldest son Samuel, you are an amazing man and because of your love and strength, we are blessed. You have become a true leader.

To my son Manuel, what an outstanding, loving and compassionate man you are! Always remember that you are someone! I know your worth.

To my daughter Elizabeth, you are my little protector. You are a dynamic woman. You helped and supported me through the abuse and in the end; I was able to bring myself out of the darkness.

Thank you for all your love and support.

Love,

Mom

THE LIE BEHIND THE BADGE

I'm sure many would like me to keep silent and stop voicing the horrible truth about what goes on behind the badge. I know I have ruffled many feathers, but I refuse to keep silent.

Many officers all over the United States and I am sure throughout the country continue to abuse their power to this day.

From Racial Profiling, to Police Brutality, and Domestic Violence this abuse of power is a serious matter within all Police Departments.

Many have hidden behind the badge, many feel they are justified for the pain they have inflicted on so many innocent people. I happen to be one of them!

For years, others would hide the truth and continue to hide what really happened to them; but the abuse of the past is shining through the dark hole of sorrow and despair.

Rosaura Torres

You cannot hide, you cannot lie. The truth does come out, and it always will in the end.

God bless you!

Carmen De La Rosa

PEACE

Many must wonder if I am bitter about the horrible abuse I endured for many years of my young adult life. I am not bitter; I am free of the abuse. Not only physical but the mental and the emotional pain I suffered by my abuser.

For years, I would hear I am sorry! It won't happen again! If you report this, I will lose my job on the police department!

I sacrificed myself to protect another human being who did not protect me! My sister and I spoke on how difficult it has been to move forward because of the memories of the abuse. I have moved forward. Why am I speaking out and telling my story? So many women, children and men are suffering because of Domestic Violence. I want to let them know, they are special, wonderful, awesome, dynamic people!!!

I prayed for years, my abuser would say, "I'm sorry". I'm sorry for what I did! I'm sorry for causing you to have eye surgery, I'm sorry for the pain I inflicted on you! I'm sorry!"

Never heard it and I never will. I no longer wait for I'm sorry. I am at PEACE. My question to my abuser, will they ever find PEACE? I pray they do because no matter what, in the now or in the later, the memory of the abuse you caused will live with you for always.

I DEDICATE THIS SHORT STORY TO MY FAMILY, MY CHILDREN, AND MY WONDERFUL FRIENDS AND TO

ALL VICTIMS AND SURVIVORS OF DOMESTIC VIOLENCE. MAY GOD BLESS ALL OF YOU.

VICTIMS AND SURVIVORS
OF
DOMESTIC VIOLENCE

To all my sister's, and brother's of Domestic Violence, I know this has been a long struggle, many feel they cannot endure anymore pain, of the horrible abuse you have sustained.

Through my training from Women in Transition, I have regained my self-confidence, my self-trust and love for myself.

My abusers were able to bend me but they did not break me. Many victims and survivors have not come out of the darkness. The horrible fact is many are still afraid of the bully who has hurt them time and time again. The BULLY who will not take responsibility for the abuse they have inflicted on their victims. We are no longer victims, we are SURVIVORS and because we survived we will speak out for JUSTICE!!!

The nightmares continue to haunt many lives. You are not alone and you will never be alone. Many are here to help you through the darkness of pain and despair. I AM HERE!!

My abusers would rather I not speak out! You will not silence me any further and to my sister's and brother's, I am here to help you through the silence. Speak out, shout from the top of the mountain and say, I am a Queen and King of God and I did not deserve the pain you inflicted upon me.

Rosaura Torres

I will continue with my battle and as I feel one day I will be victorious, so will you! Someone once said, "I have the will to survive and so will you"!!

God bless all my victims and survivors of DOMESTICE VIOLENCE

LOVE AND RESPECT,

CARMEN DE LA ROSA

TO ALL MY HEROS

Today is another day, today is a positive day, and today is a day to THANK all my hero's, advocates, writers, supporters, victims, and survivors.

I am honored to know every one of you! You are the positive voice many need to hear, you are the helping hand, many reach out too! You are a brilliant light at the end of the darkness.

I know as far as Australia, Canada, Spain, Puerto Rico, and all over United States, we have so many WONDERFUL HERO'S who are extending their loving hands. God has given every one of you a SHIELD OF ARMOUR.

Keep your heads high and continue with positive confidence.
So today is a day for all HERO'S ALL OVER THE WORLD.
Thank you, for all your love and support. May you continue to be the BEACON of light and love God has always meant for you to be.

With love and respect,

CARMEN DE LA ROSA

239

BLESSED

A year ago, I was blessed to find a friend and an angel. I will call her Star.

Through my young adult life, I watched and listened to how a family can be so controlling, because of their controlling ways Star became of victim of DOMESTIC VIOLENCE.

When she tried to confide in family about the abuse, the family questioned Star, they did not believe she was being abused.

Why, do so many families and friends question a victim about being abused? I remember like it was yesterday, when my family member said to me, "what did you do to him for him to hit you?"

How can you question a victim of abuse about what their abuser did to them?

Star and I have lost each other again, but the respect and love I have for her will be with me always!

My past abusers were not able to silence me. My past abusers could not get to most of the family, but they got to Star.
To all victims and survivors of domestic violence, there are some family, some friends, who will become angry because your voice is being heard. You are telling the truth, it is because you refuse to hide and protect someone who did not protect you!

You are not alone; God is right by your side as well as those who truly love and respect you.

To the Star's in this great world, I love you always!

Rosaura Torres

God Bless You,

Carmen De La Rosa

I WALK WITH GOD

Please forgive me for what I am about to write. I am responsible for so much pain my ex-husband and I caused to our sons.

My sons were victims of Domestic Violence and it was wrong. No justification will erase any pain or damage which was caused.

For the past eleven years, I have expressed to my sons repeatedly that living with this abuse was wrong. There is no excuse, it was wrong. I was wrong.

I will take full responsibility because as their mother I did not protect them, as I should have. I have been reminded of the hurt my ex-husband and I have caused to our sons.

I remember when my son was a teenager and his father beat him like a man in front of several police officers'; I am to blame for what happened. As his mother, I should have been able to stop it.

I have prayed to God for forgiveness, repeatedly. I have prayed for him to help me to help others and I prayed for my sons' forgiveness.
My love for my children is unconditional. I hang my head low because I continued through the cycle of abuse; all the while, I loved them the best way I knew how.

For those who are without sin, cast the first stone. I am with sin and I am deeply sorry for all the pain my sons have endured.

My daughter, I gave you my life; I love you and my grandchildren so deeply and I ignored the abuse, which continued, in our home.

I will never disown you or your brothers; you are my blood and my love, but I must stop the cycle or I will also be held responsible for the continued cycle of abuse.

I walk with God. When my time comes, I walk with God. I will not take you with me and I will wait for the time when God decides for me to walk with him.

To my three children …I love you more than you will ever know and I pray that one day we will come together again as a family.

To my past abuser, no matter what damage has been caused, it is my memory and my choice to tell my story. Our children have nothing to do with this.

I wish you all the blessings in the world, but please do not try to prevent me from helping others.

Mary Magdalene was judged and almost stoned until Jesus stopped people from stoning her.

To my friends and supporters, I ask you to forgive me please; I was wrong.

God bless each and every one of you,

Carmen De La Rosa

A Latino Literacy Now &
Latino Book & Family Festival Awards Program

THE 2011 INTERNATIONAL LATINO BOOK AWARDS

In the category of
BEST WOMEN'S ISSUES BOOK - ENGLISH

Abuse Hidden Behind The Badge
Rosaura Torres

TORRES PUBLISHING GROUP, LLC

Is Awarded
FIRST PLACE

The International Latino Book Awards Celebration   May 25, 2011
El Museo del Barrio, 1230 Fifth Ave., New York City

243

Made in the USA
Charleston, SC
26 April 2012